Applied Math Series

METRICS AT WORK

BY JOHN L.P. MCCABE

COVER DESIGN BY KATHY KIFER

A Breath of Fresh Air

Garlic Press

Dedicated to
The World of Metrics.

Published by:
Garlic Press
100 Hillview Lane #2
Eugene, OR 97408

ISBN 0-931993-70-9
Order Number GP-070

Table of Contents

INTRODUCTION

Standards of weights and measures have varied down through the ages. In primitive times, weights and measures were based on the most familiar elements of nature: body parts (arms, hands, fingers) for length; heavenly bodies (the sun and moon) for time; and seeds and stones for mass and weight.

As societies evolved, measurement became more complex. The invention of numbering systems and mathematics made it possible to create more accurate systems of measurement suited to trade and commerce, land division, taxation, and scientific research. But because of their geographic isolation from one another, different cultures and regions often developed their own standards.

The push for a single worldwide measurement system was fostered by the French government in the late eighteenth century. Countries around the world began to support France's efforts, and the result is today's International System of Units, abbreviated SI for the French *Le Systeme International d'Unites*.

SI Metrics is a decimal-based system (similar to our decimal money system) that is both simple and scientific. All units of measurement are organized in factors of 10: 10s, 100s, 1,000s, etc. Because of this, calculations with metric units often involve simply moving a decimal point to the right or left. There is no adding or subtracting of cumbersome fractions. There are also no internal conversion factors, such as 12 inches in a foot, 16 ounces in a pound, or 32 fluid ounces in a quart.

SI Metrics has only seven basic units, one for each type of quantity. For example, instead of inch, foot, yard, and mile, the meter is the only metric unit for the measurement of length. Longer and shorter lengths are made by multiplying or dividing the meter by factors of 10. Two examples are kilometers (one thousand meters) and the millimeter (one-thousandth of a meter).

The most common metric units in everyday use are: for length, the meter (and its multiples from millimeter to kilometer); for weight or mass, the gram (and its multiples from milligram to kilogram); for volume, the liter (and its multiples from milliliter to kiloliter); and for temperature, the degree Celsius.

SI Metrics has come to be the international standard of measurement for most of the world, and for good reason. As nations interact more and more in a global marketplace, the need for common standards and specifications for products, machinery, tools, and parts becomes tantamount. SI Metrics, with its simple "base 10" system, fills this need well.

Interestingly, the United States is the only industrial nation that does not require SI Metrics for general use. The English System (also known as the Customary System or the "inch-pound system") remains the preferred system for most Americans. But as the use of SI Metrics inevitably increases throughout the world, it is essential that Americans learn how to use it correctly so the U.S. can remain competitive in the global marketplace.

Metrics at Work has been written to provide a method for learning SI Metrics and applying it to daily activities and commerce. Further, **Metrics at Work** provides comparisons and conversions between SI Metrics and the English System of measurement. A step-by-step approach to problem solving is used throughout this book. This approach was selected to allow readers to work at their own pace and to absorb and comprehend the material as they progress.

Metrics at Work is acceptable for students of all ages. Those in early elementary grades through college years can use it to learn about SI Metrics and English System conversions.

John L. P. McCabe

Chapter 1
Conversions Between Systems

This chapter will offer instruction on converisons and comparisons between two systems of measurement—English and SI Metrics.

The English System of Measurement

The English System is the system commonly used in the United States . It is nearly the same as that brought by the colonists from England. The units of measure in the English System have their origins in a variety of cultures—Babylonian, Egyptian, Roman, Anglo-Saxon, and Norman-French.

It is not suprising, then, that the English System is an eclectic mix of units that originally had nothing to do with one another but now are linked by various conversion factors. For example, the length of a furlong (or furrow-long) was established by early Tudor rulers as 220 yards. This led Queen Elizabeth to declare in the 16th century that thenceforth, the traditional Roman mile of 5,000 feet would be replaced by one of 5,280 feet, making the mile exactly 8 furlongs and providing a convenient relationship between two previously ill-related measures.

Despite continuing to use the English System, the United States has been involved in the development of the SI Metrics system since its beginnings in the late 18th century. In fact, all traditional U.S. units have been based on metric units since 1893. (For example, an inch is defined as exactly 2.54 centimeters). And in 1959, U.S. length units (inch, foot, yard, mile, etc.) were even shortened slightly to make them simpler multiples of the meter.

Emphasis for Change

As other English-speaking countries adopted SI Metrics in the 1960s and 1970s, the United States prepared to do so as well with the 1975 Metric Conversion Act. A few major industries converted, but many people resisted. Some opposed SI because they felt it was un-American. Others feared that conversion would be too difficult or expensive. Under pressure from various groups, the U.S. Congress made the use of SI Metrics voluntary, and the metric transition process lost momentum.

In the 1980s, it became increasingly apparent that Americans' adherence to the English System was eroding their ability to compete in the global marketplace, where SI Metrics had become the standard. Progressive business and educational leaders urged the government to mandate SI Metrics once and for all, in the belief that doing so would increase the United States' exports and improve its balance of trade, ultimately leading to a higher standard of living. In 1988, the U.S. Congress establsihed SI Metrics as the preferred system for U.S trade and commerce, and required all federal agencies to adopt it, to the extent economically feasible, by the end of 1992. In 1991 then-President George Bush issued an Executive Order, "Metric Usage in Federal Government Programs," further strengthening the push toward metrics.

But don't throw away your yardstick or ruler or scales or measuring pitchers just yet. Some domestic industries in the U.S. may never change from the English System of measurement because conversion is still NOT mandatory. However, those doing business with the federal government must now produce goods using metric measure.

The change-over should not be severely felt by most citizens of the U.S. Packages and cartons will generally display both SI and customary units of measure for an extended period of time. This method will allow consumers and students to become familiar with comparing units of measure.

The "dual" system of measurement is already in use in some industries. Check the next can of soda, carton of milk, or can of motor oil that you buy. A can of soda might show "12 Fl Oz/354 mL". A carton of milk or can of oil might show "1 quart/.946 L." Bakers rejoice! Flour may be sold by kilograms (kg) of weight, but teaspoons, tablespoons, and cups will remain in recipes.

Explore with Us

Be patient with yourself as we explore, together, the world of SI Metrics. You will be learning a new "language" of measurement. Time and patience on your part will be necessary to make the transition understandable and perhaps enjoyable, too.

Noticeable changes will generally occur in LENGTH measurements: kilometer (km), meter (m), centimeter (cm), and millimeter (mm), instead of miles, yards or feet, inches, and fractions of an inch.

WEIGHT or MASS measurements will become kilograms (kg), grams (g), and milligrams (mg) instead of tons, pounds and ounces.

CAPACITY measurements will change to liters (L), and milliliters (mL), instead of gallons, quarts and pints.

TEMPERATURE measurements will be reported and displayed in degrees Celsius (C) instead of degrees Fahrenheit (F).

TIME measurement has always been the same internationally and will not change. And, the U.S. MONETARY system (money) will also remain unchanged.

Those who "grew up" with the English System of measurement will be constantly comparing it to SI Metrics to get a clearer picture. Visualize that 1 meter (m) is just over 39 inches in length or a little over a yard long, 1 kilometer (km) is about 5/8 of a mile in length, 1 inch equals 2.54 centimeters (cm), and 1 inch also equals 25.4 millimeters (mm), 28 grams (g) equal about 1 ounce, 1 liter (L) equals just over a quart, and 1° Celsius (C) equals about 2° Fahrenheit (F). Take time to become familiar with these important comparisons.

Converting English and SI Metric Systems

The Conversion Chart and Conversion Values shown below outline common comparisons between the two systems of measurement.

CONVERSION CHART
(approximate values)

METRIC TO ENGLISH

LENGTH

TO CONVERT FROM	TO	MULTIPLY BY
millimeters	inches	0.039
centimeters	inches	0.39
meters	inches	39.37
meters	feet	3.28
meters	yards	1.09
kilometers	miles	0.62

AREA

FROM	TO	=
sq. centimeters	sq. in.	0.155
sq. meters	sq. ft.	10.763
sq. meters	sq. yds.	1.2
sq. kilometers	sq. mi.	0.4

MASS (WEIGHT)

FROM	TO	=
grams	ounces	0.035
kilograms	pounds	2.205
ton	pounds	2205.

VOLUME

FROM	TO	=
cubic cm.	cu. in.	0.061
cubic meters	cu. yds.	1.308
milliliters	fl. oz.	0.033
liters	fl. oz.	33.814
liters	pints	2.113
liters	quarts	1.056
liters	gallons	0.264

TEMPERATURE

FROM	TO	=
Celsius	Fahrenheit	$\frac{9(C+32)}{5}$

ENGLISH TO METRIC

LENGTH

TO CONVERT FROM	TO	MULTIPLY BY
inches	millimeters	25.4
inches	centimeters	2.54
inches	meters	0.0254
feet	meters	0.304
yards	meters	0.914
miles	kilometers	1.609

AREA

FROM	TO	=
sq. in.	sq. centimeters	6.451
sq. ft.	sq. meters	0.092
sq. yd.	sq. meters	0.8
sq. mi.	sq. kilometers	2.6

MASS (WEIGHT)

FROM	TO	=
ounces	grams	28.35
pounds	kilograms	0.453
tons	kilograms	907.2

VOLUME

FROM	TO	=
cu. in.	cubic cm.	16.387
cu. yd.	cubic meters	0.764
fl. oz.	milliliters	29.574
fl. oz.	liters	0.029
pints	liters	0.473
quarts	liters	0.946
gallons	liters	3.785

TEMPERATURE

FROM	TO	=
Fahrenheit	Celsius	$\frac{5(F-32)}{9}$

CONVERTED VALUES

(approximate values)

METRIC   **ENGLISH**

MEASURES OF LENGTH

METRIC		=	ENGLISH	
1.0	millimeter		0.03937	inch
1.0	centimeter		0.3937	inch
1.0	meter		39.37	inches
1.0	meter		3.28	feet
1.0	meter		1.093	yards
1.0	kilometer		.6214	miles
25.4	millimeters		1.0	inch
2.54	centimeters		1.0	inch
.304	meters		1.0	foot
.914	meters		1.0	yard
1.609	kilometers		1.0	mile

MEASURES OF WEIGHT

METRIC		=	ENGLISH	
1.0	kilogram		2.2	pounds
1.0	gram		0.035	ounces
.907	metric ton		1.102	tons
28.35	grams		1.0	ounce
453.0	grams		1.0	pound

MEASURES OF CAPACITY

METRIC		=	ENGLISH	
1.0	liter L (1 cubic decimeter)		61.023	cubic inches
			0.03521	cubic feet
			.2642	gallons
			1.06	dry quarts
3.785	liters		1.0	gallon
28.317	liters		1.0	cubic foot
29.574	milliliters		1.0	fl. ounce
473.18	milliliters		1.0	fl. pint
946.35	milliliters		1.0	fl. quart

MEASURES OF TEMPERATURE

METRIC	=	ENGLISH
0° Celsius C	(water freezes)	32° Fahrenheit
100° Celsius C	(water boils)	212° Fahrenheit

Exercise 1 Conversions Between Systems

This exercise will offer the opportunity to put the proceding charts to use. Convert the following English and Metric measurements.

Example:

> Convert 5 meters (m) to feet.
>
> SOLUTION:
>
> The chart shows that 1 meter equals 3.28 feet.
>
> 5 x 3.28 = 16.4 feet.

1. 10 cm = _____ inches

2. 18 m = _____ yards

3. 5 yards = _____ m

4. 25 km = _____ miles

5. 10 miles = _____ km

6. 20 m = _____ feet

7. 7 m = _____ inches

8. 10 kg = _____ pounds

9. 3 gallons = _____ liters

10. 5 inches = _____ cm

11. 3 feet = _____ m

12. 7 km = _____ miles

13. 10 cm = _____ inches

14. 70° F = _____ °C

15. 24 ounces = _____ grams

16. 20 inches = _____ mm

17. 7 feet = _____ meters

18. 10 liters = _____ qt.

19. 20° C = _____ °F

20. 15 feet = _____ m

21. 1'6" = _____ cm

22. 10 feet = _____ mm

23. 7.62 cm = _____ inches

24. 36" = _____ m

The story problems to follow are just simply conversion problems with words added to make them more interesting (round answers to the third decimal place).

Example:

> It is 7'0" to the top of our neighbor's fence. How many meters (m) does that equal?
>
> SOLUTION:
>
> The Conversion Chart converts feet to meters—multiply by .304.
>
> $7 \times .304 = 2.128$ m

1. A flag pole is 32 feet tall. How many meters (m) does this equal?

_____ m

2. Jim is running in a 10K race next week. How many miles does this equal? (10K is the same as 10 km.)

_____ miles

3. An oval dirt race tract is $\frac{3}{4}$ mile in length. How many kilometers (km) does this represent?

_____ km

4. Mary purchased 3 quarts of milk along with other food items. How many liters (L) does this represent?

_____ L

5. A bolt of cloth is 42 inches wide. How many centimeters (cm) does this equal?

_____ cm

6. A load of firewood weighed 750 pounds. How many kilograms (kg) does this equal?

_____ kg

7. Our Fahrenheit thermometer registered 50° at 7 A.M. this morning. What is the equivalent temperature on the Celsius scale?

_____ C

8. Our cat, Rufus, weighs 7.5 pounds. How many grams (g) does Rufus weigh?

_____ g

9. A large pizza is approximately 37" in circumference. How many centimeters (cm) does this equal?

_____ cm

10. Seven liters (L) equals how many pints?

_____ pints

11. A 20K (kilometer) cross-country relay race is being run next Saturday. There are four runners on each team. Approximately how many feet will each team member run?

_____ feet

12. The church steeple in our village is 25 meters (m) tall. Approximately how many feet does this equal?

_____ feet

13. The gas tank in my Oldsmobile holds 14 gallons of gasoline. Approximately how many liters (L) does this equal?

_____ liters

14. My weight is 160 pounds. Approximately how many grams (g) and kilograms (kg) does this equal?

_____ g

_____ kg

15. A piece of 2"x4" yellow pine is 8'0" long. It is to be cut into 3—2'6" pieces. Disregard cutting waste, and determine how many centimeters (cm) will be left.

_____ cm

16. A piece of steel angle iron is 4'2" long. Approximately how many centimeters (cm) does this equal?

_____ cm

17. A diesel-powered freight train travels 70 km in one hour. Approximately how many miles does the train travel in 2 hours?

_____ miles

18. The total weight of a package to be mailed is 6 pounds. Approximately how many grams (g) does this equal?

_____ g

19. A new home being built in our neighborhood has one bedroom that measures 10'0" x 12'0" in size. How many square feet and how many square meters does this equal?

_____ sq. ft.

_____ sq. m

20. A standard city block is 600 feet long. Approximately how many meters (m) does this equal?

_____ m

This chapter provided an opportunity for you to get acquainted with conversions between the two systems of measurement. And as a "bonus" you worked story problems, too. Congratulations! Chapter 1 will provide a handy reference for you. Keep it available. With proper preparation, the path ahead will be less difficult to travel.

Chapter 2

Length Measurements

This chapter will introduce you to metric length measurements. You will also learn how to convert between different length units. Developing skills to convert between units is crucial to your future success as you are introduced to other metric measurements in subsequent chapters.

The **meter** is the basic unit of metric length. Other units of length that are commonly used are the kilometer (km), decimeter (dm), centimeter (cm), and millimeter (mm). More about the hectometer (hm) and the dekameter (dam) later.

Let's compare the simple metric length units. Here is a Metric Value Chart which compares all unit lengths relative to the meter (the "basic" unit).

Metric Value Chart 1 • Length Measurement

Unit	Kilometer	Hectometer	Dekameter	Basic Unit Meter	Decimeter	Centimeter	Millimeter
Symbol	1 km =	1 hm =	1 dam =	1 m =	1 dm =	1 cm =	1 mm =
Base Unit Value	1000 m	100 m	10 m	1 m	0.1 m	0.01 m	0.001 m

Prefixes added to a **basic unit** (meter, liter, gram) create larger or smaller units by factors that are powers of 10.

Prefix =	Kilo	Hecto	Deka	Basic Unit	Deci	Centi	Milli
	thousand	hundred	ten		tenth	hundredth	thousandth
	x Basic Unit	x Basic Unit	x Basic Unit		x Basic Unit	x Basic Unit	x Basic Unit

Converting Units — Moving the Decimal

Use the Metric Value Chart as a guide and you will discover that conversion between units occurs easily by moving the decimal point.

Examples:

Convert (a) 9 m to cm, (b) 47 m to mm, and (c) 4.5 cm to mm.

SOLUTIONS:

a. Place a decimal point to the right of 9 m. Now move the decimal point TWO places to the RIGHT because centimeter is TWO places to the RIGHT of meters on the Metric Value Chart.

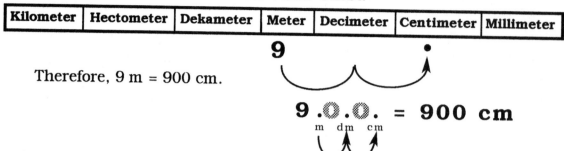

Kilometer	Hectometer	Dekameter	Meter	Decimeter	Centimeter	Millimeter

Therefore, 9 m = 900 cm.

9 .0.0. = 900 cm

To convert 900 cm back to meters, place a decimal point to the RIGHT of 900. Now move the decimal point TWO places to the LEFT because meters are TWO places to the left of centimeters on the Metric Value Chart. Therefore, 900 cm = 9 m (The decimal point is removed because there are no digits to the right of the decimal point.)

9 .0.0. = 9 m

b. To convert 47 m to mm, move the decimal THREE places to the RIGHT. 47 m = 47 000 mm.

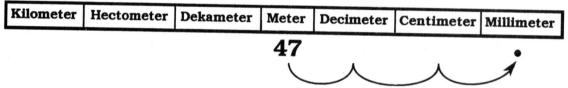

Kilometer	Hectometer	Dekameter	Meter	Decimeter	Centimeter	Millimeter

Another conversion: Convert 47 000 mm to km. Move the decimal point SIX places to the LEFT because kilometer is SIX places to the LEFT of millimeter on the Metric Value line. 47 000 mm = .047 m

c. To convert 4.5 cm to mm, move the decimal point ONE place to the RIGHT because millimeter is ONE place to the RIGHT on the Metric Value Chart. 4.5 cm = 45 mm.

Another conversion: Convert 45 mm to meters. Move the decimal point THREE places to the LEFT because meter is 3 places to the LEFT on the Metric Value Chart. 45 mm = .045 m.

Refer to the Metric Value Chart. Recognize this relationship: .009 km = .09 hm or .9 dam or 9 m or 90 dm or 900 cm or 9 000 mm. All of these notations were reached be moving the decimal point to the RIGHT. All have the same value! They all measure the same distance.

The Metric Value Chart is a helpful guide for your use and reference. You will be presented with other, similar charts as you work with other metric measurements.

It is important to mention that hectometers (hm) and dekameters (dam) are not commonly used metric length meaurements. They are brought to your attention to show their relationship to other units on the Metric Value Chart. Your attention and interest should be directed to kilometer (km), meter (m), decimeter (dm), centimeter (cm) and millimeter (mm).

The Metric Value Chart is a great beginning "tool" to help you convert between metric measurements. However, after some experience, you will use the Metric Value Chart less and less. Remember the training wheels on your first sidewalk bike? And how anxious you were to discard them? You will eventually feel the same way about the Metric Value Chart.

Exercise ❶ Converting Units of Length

You've been studying the Metric Value Chart and how it works when converting between units of length. Now you have an opportunity to test your skills by working the following problems:

1. 10 m = _____ cm

2. 5 cm = _____ mm

3. 25 cm = _____ mm

4. 100 mm = _____ m

5. 165 mm = _____ m

6. 5 mm = _____ km

7. 500 km = _____ m

8. 700 cm = _____ km

9. 7 km = _____ m

10. 35.5 cm = _____ m

11. 7 000 km = _____ m

12. 50 dm = _____ hm

13. 750 m = _____ km

14. 1 500 cm = _____ m

15. 50 m = _____ cm

16. 600 dm = _____ km

Work problems 17 thru 26 by FIRST converting to common units, then add, subtract, or multiply as required.

Example:

4 mm + 1 cm = _____ m (Convert 4 mm to .004 m and 1 cm to .01 m before adding.)
.004 m + .01 m = <u>.014</u> m (Line up the decimal points.)

17. 5 m + 10 cm = _____ mm

18. 35 m - 20 dm = _____ cm

19. 7 km x 5 = _____ m

20. 150 m x 2.5 = _____ cm

21. 3 cm x 5 mm = _____ mm

22. 7.5 mm x 9 cm = _____ mm

23. 6 m x 5 = _____ cm

24. 5 m - 10 cm = _____ m

25. 9 m + 2 cm - 5 mm = _____ cm

26. 5 x 2 m = _____ cm

11

Exercise ❷ Applying Conversions

Work the length and distance problems that follow.

1. Here is a metric ruler. The numbers indicate centimeters. Give the length in centimeters from the beginning of the ruler to each letter.

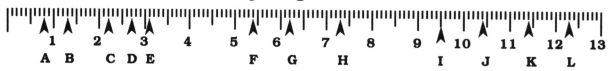

A =   B =   C =   D =

E =   F =   G =   H =

I =   J =   K =   L =

2. Measure the approximate length of the lines shown here:

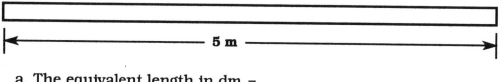

A = _____   B = _   C = _____   D = ___
    cm   mm   cm   mm

3. The piece of pipe shown here is 5 meters (m) long.

|←—————————— 5 m ——————————→|

    a. The equivalent length in dm = _____

    b. The equivalent length in cm = _____

    c. The equivalent length in mm = _____

Here are some complex length and distance problems. Remember to make the appropriate conversions to arrive at the required unit of measurement.

4. Determine the missing dimensions.

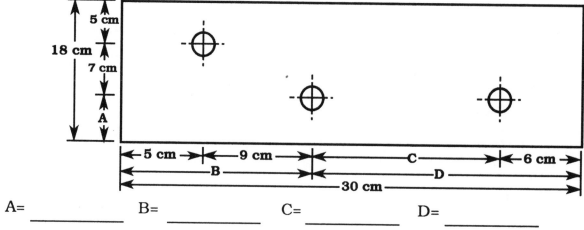

A= _____   B= _____   C= _____   D= _____

12

5. Determine dimension A in meters (m).

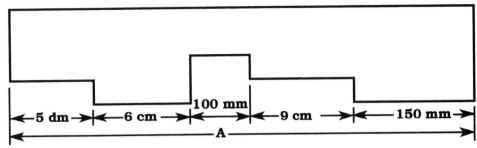

A= _____ m

6. Five pieces of steel pipe are welded together as shown. Determine the length of A in the units required.

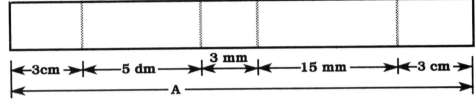

a. A = _____ millimeters (mm)   b. A = _____ centimeters (cm)

c. A = _____ decimeters (dm)   d. A = _____ meters (m)

7. How many total kilometers (km) does a car travel in 7 hours of driving at the average speed of 80 km/hour?

_____ km

8. A speed of 80 km/hour equals approximately how many mph? (Check the Conversion Chart in Chapter 1.)

_____ mph

9. In problem #7 above, approximately how many miles are driven in the 7-hours driving time?

_____ miles

10. Refer to problem #7 above and determine how many meters are driven in 7-hours of driving time.

_____ meters

11. Solve the following mixed operations:

a. 4 m + 25 cm + 90 mm = _____ cm

b. 5.5 cm + 2.5 m - 10 cm = _____ mm

c. 15 m x 5 cm + 10 m = _____ m

d. 15 m - 10 cm + 10 mm = _____ m

13

e. 5 m x 6 m + 20 cm = _____ cm

f. 200 mm + 25 cm + 50 dm = _____ cm

g. 10 mm x 5 cm = _____ cm

Refer to the charts in Chapter 1 when working the following problems:

12. If there are 25.4 millimeters (mm) in 1 inch, how many meters (m) are in 9'6"?

_____ m

13. Jim Brown is 2 meters (m) tall. How many inches does this equal?

_____ "

14. It's been established that Jim Brown is 2 meters (m) tall, how many centimeters (cm) does this equal?

_____ cm

15. The Chugwater County race track is $1\frac{1}{4}$ miles long. How many kilometers (km) does this equal?

_____ km

16. The neighboring community of High Point is 20 kilometers (km) away. How many meters (m) would this equal?

_____ m

17. A 5K walkathon is scheduled for seniors in our town. How many meters (m) does this equal?

_____ m

18. On a recent cross-country automobile trip, the distance between two cities was 32 miles. How many kilometers (km) does this equal?

_____ km

19. A steel beam shown here has a total length of 5 meters (m). Five pieces are welded together. Determine the missing length.

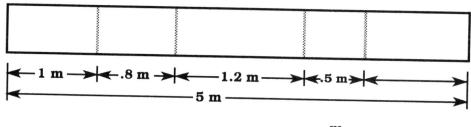

_____ m

14

20. A milled steel bushing measures 20 mm in length. The Uptown Machine Shop has an order for 15,000 bushings. Disregard cutting loss and determine how many meters (m) of material are required.

_____ m

21. The fishing pier at Gun Lake is .5 km long and is located on the south shore of the lake. How many meters (m) does this equal?

_____ m

22. A square-shaped 80-acre farm measures approximately 1867 feet on each side. How many meters (m) does this equal?

_____ m

23. The best fishing place at Gun Lake is said to be about 360 feet deep. How many meters (m) does this equal?

_____ m

24. My uncle caught a wide-mouth bass at Gun Lake that measured 14 inches long. How many centimeters (cm) does this equal?

_____ cm

25. A beautiful and productive Iowa farm near the city of Waverly is one mile square and consists of 640 acres. The farm is cross-fenced into 8 equal fields of 80 acres each.

a. How many kilometers (km) do each of the four sides of the 640 acre farm measure?

_____ km

b. How many meters (m) of fencing are required around the perimeter of the 640 acre farm?

_____ m

c. How many meters (m) of cross-fencing are required?

_____ m

d. How many feet of cross-fencing does this equal?

_____ ft.

15

e. Each 80 acre field is 1320 feet wide and 2640 feet long. How many meters (m) does each of these dimensions equal?

_____ meters wide

_____ meters long

f. How many meters are on each side of the 640 acre farm?

_____ m

g. How many total feet of perimeter fencing and cross-fencing are required for the farm?

_____ ft.

Chapter 3
Square Measurement

This chapter will present examples and problems in square measure. Square measure is more accurately a length measurement of area. And since area has 2-dimensions, we speak of area as 'squared.' The basic unit of square measurement is still the meter, but the square meter (m^2).

The prefixes we learned with simple length reflected the power of 10 and the decimal point was moved ONE place at a time. The decimal movement for square measurements now reflect powers of 100 and movement is TWO places at a time.

To show you how square measurement is influenced by the movement of the decimal to the powers of 100, here is another Metric Value Chart. It shows how a square meter changes to become equivalent to a square kilometer, square hectometer, square dekameter, square decimeter, square centimeter, and square millimeter.

Metric Value Chart 2 • Square Measurement

Unit	Kilometer	Hectometer	Dekameter	Basic Unit Meter	Decimeter	Centimeter	Millimeter
Symbol	1 sq. km =	1 sq. hm =	1 sq. dam =	1 sq. m	1 sq. dm =	1 sq. cm =	1 sq. mm =
Base Unit Value	1 000 000 sq. m	10 000 sq. m	100 sq. m	1 sq. m	0.01 m	0.0001 sq. m	0.000001 sq. m

Converting Units — Like Terms & Moving the Decimal

When you work with measurements to determine area, you must first convert all simple measurements to like terms. You can then proceed to determine the area (square measure).

Example:

> What is the area of a rectangle where side A = 5 dm and side B = 10 cm?
>
> SOLUTION:
>
> Convert to like terms — Change 5 dm to 50 cm. (Refer to a Metric Value Chart to convert)
>
> Multiply like terms using the formula for a rectangle:
>
> A = l · w
> A = 50 cm x 10 cm
> A = 500 sq. cm

Suppose you are required to convert between units of square measure ?

Example:

What is the area of a rectangle where side A = 5 dm and side B = 10 cm? Express your answer in square millimeters.

SOLUTION:

We have already determined the answer as 500 sq. cm. We merely need to convert from sq. cm to sq. mm.

Square Kilometer	Square Hectometer	Square Dekameter	Square Meter	Square Decimeter	Square Centimeter	Square Millimeter

Remember for square measurements, the decimal moves TWO places per square unit.

500 sq. cm

5 0 0 . 0 0 . = **50 000 sq. mm**
sq. cm   sq. mm

Exercise ❶ Applying Conversions

1. Four pieces of wood are in stock in a storage area. Piece A has a top surface area of 20 sq. dm, Piece B has a top surface area of 3 sq. m, Piece C has a top surface area of 150 sq. cm, and Piece D has a top surface area of 4 sq. dm. What is the total top surface area for all the wood in sq. dm?

   I'll help you get started! First convert Piece B and Piece C to sq. dm.
   Piece A = 20 sq. dm
   Piece B = 3 sq. m or 300 sq. dm (3 x 100)
   Piece C = 150 sq. cm or 1.5 sq. dm (decimal point moves 2 places to the left)
   Piece D = 4 sq. dm

   The conversion to sq. dm has been completed. Now total all individual lengths.

   _____ sq. dm

2. How many sq. mm are contained in the area of a rectangle which has side A equaling 8 cm and side B equaling 10 dm? First convert side B to cm. by moving the decimal point 1 place to the right to get 100 cm. Now multiply side A by side B to get sq. cm. Convert sq. cm to sq. mm.

   _____ sq. mm

3. A welder needs 250 sq. cm of steel plate to do a job. There are four pieces of steel plate in stock. The areas of each: A = 50 sq. cm, B = 2 sq. dm, C = 100 sq. mm, and piece D has 100 sq. cm. How many sq. cm are in stock?

   _____ sq. cm

4. What is the total area in sq. dm of the following pieces of plywood? Piece A = 2 sq. m, B = 4.5 sq. dm, and C = 300 sq. cm. Convert all measures to sq. dm before proceeding.

_____ sq. dm

5. A piece of plywood has a rectangular shape with dimensions of 15 cm on one side and 12 cm on the other side.

   a. Find the area in sq. cm   _____ sq. cm

   b. Find the area in sq. mm   _____ sq. mm

   c. Find the area in sq. dm   _____ sq. dm

   d. Find the area in sq. m   _____ sq. m

6. Each of thrity (30) rectangular pieces of metal measures 2 dm on one side and 5 dm on the other side.

   a. Find the total area of 30 pieces in sq. m   _____ sq. m

   b. Find the total area of 30 pieces in sq. dm   _____ sq. dm

7. A small farm on the edge of town is square in shape, measuring 200 m on each side. What is the total area in sq. hm? (There are at least two ways to solve this problem. Change 200 m to hm and square the sides or square the 200 m dimension and convert your answer to hm.)

_____ sq. hm

8. A bolt of cloth is cut into 500 pieces. Each piece is 5 cm by 20 cm. What is the total area of all 500 pieces in sq. m?

_____ sq. m

9. Add the pieces of canvas described here and convert the total area to sq. m.

Piece A (500 pieces) 10 cm x 15 cm

Piece B (200 pieces) 5 cm x 5 cm

_____ sq. m

10. The Downtown Parking Garage is 20 m wide and 60 m long. Thirty per cent of the floor area is used for the driving lane. How much space in sq. m remains for parking cars? (70% of the total floor area is used for parking cars.)

_____ sq. m

19

11. A rectangular piece of aluminum measures 1.5 m on the short side and 3.5 m on the long side. Three circles are cut from this sheet:

Circle A has a diameter of 1 dm
Circle B has a diameter of 30 cm
Circle C has a diameter of 1.5 dm

   a. What is the area of the flat piece of aluminum in sq. m before the cutouts are made?

_____ sq. m

   b. What is the area in sq. cm of circle A?

_____ sq. cm

   c. What is the area in sq. dm of circle B?

_____ sq. dm

   d. What is the area in sq. mm of circle C?

_____ sq. mm

   e. With the circle cutouts removed, what is the remaining area in sq. cm of the piece of flat aluminum?

_____ sq. cm

12. Monument Park measures 8 dam on the short side and 10 dam on the long side. Determine the total area in sq. m.

_____ sq. m

13. The circular milking parlor on my uncle's farm is 13 m in diameter and will accommodate 8 cows at a time. How many sq. m does the circular milking parlor cover?

_____ sq. m

14. When the sun is directly overhead, the shadow cast by our 70-year old, perfectly shaped maple tree is 40 feet across (diameter). How many sq. m would be in the shaded circle?

_____ sq. m

15. Our patio measures 8 m on one side and 4 m on the other side. How many sq. dm are in the patio?

_____ sq. dm

16. A flower garden has the dimensions shown here. The entire plot is divided into planting areas as noted: Areas 1 & 2 = Area 3, Areas 4 & 5 = Area 6. Area 6 is twice the size of Area 3. Determine the area in sq. m of each planting area.

2m **3**	**2**	**1**
4 m **6**	**5** 3 m	**4** 3 m

6 m

12 m

Area 1 = _____ sq. m

Area 2 = _____ sq. m

Area 3 = _____ sq. m

Area 4 = _____ sq. m

Area 5 = _____ sq. m

Area 6 = _____ sq. m

17. The walls and ceiling of our living room will be repainted using an off-white paint. The plan of the room is shown here. Window and door areas are to be deducted from surfaces to be painted. Ceiling height is 2.44 m. 3.8 L of paint covers 37 square meters of surface area.

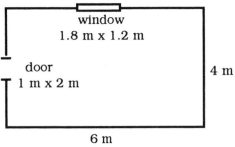

window
1.8 m x 1.2 m

door
1 m x 2 m

4 m

6 m

a. How many sq. m of surface will be painted?

_____ sq. m

b. How many liters (L) of paint will be required?

_____ L

18. The plot of land shown here is divided into 5 equal lots. What is the area in sq. m of each lot?

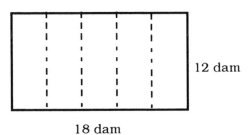

12 dam

18 dam

_____ sq. m

19. Twelve steel gussets shaped as right triangles are used in the construction of a home for corner reinforcing. The dimensions of the triangle are 14 cm and 10 cm as shown here. Two gussets together would represent a rectangle 14 cm by 10 cm.)

14 cm

10 cm

What is the length and width of the plate required for the 12 cuts? (Assume no cutting loss.)

_____

20. The gazebo in our neighbor's yard has the dimensions shown. The wood deck is showing some wear and the owners have decided to cover the deck with outdoor carpet which will be cemented in place.

Note: Each flat side = 2 m

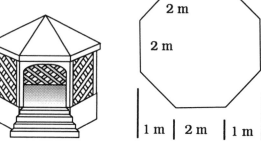

2 m

2 m

1 m | 2 m | 1 m

Determine the number of sq. m of outdoor carpet required to cover the deck.

_____ sq. m

21. The concrete driveway in front of our garage measures 6 m wide by 10 m long. Determine the area in sq. dam.

_____ sq. dam

22. My mother's favorite cake pan is 4 cm wide and 6 cm long. How many sq. mm does the pan contain?

_____ sq. mm

Chapter 4

Volume Measurement-Cubic Capacity

This chapter will present examples and problems in cubic measure. Cubic measure is more accurately a length measurement of volume. And since volume has 3-dimensions, we speak of volume as 'cubed.' The basic unit of measurement is still the meter, but the cubic meter (m^3).

Decimal movement between cubic units is THREE places. Thus, cubic decimal movements are powers of 1000.

Converting Units Like Terms & Moving the Decimal

The procedure for solving problems involving cubic measure is similar to that learned for square measure (Chapter 3). Convert all measurements to like terms. Then proceed to determine volume (cubic measure) and make any conversions between units as necessary.

Example:

> Determine the volume of a box in cubic decimeters with sides of 10 cm, 2 dm, and 5 cm.
>
> SOLUTIONS:
>
> **Method A**
> Convert all measurements to centimeters (Remember Metric Value Chart 1). Use the standard volume formula Volume (V) = length (L) x width (W) x height (H). Convert calculated answer to appropriate cubic measure.
>
> Convert to like terms: Side A = 10 cm = 10 cm
> Side B = 2 dm = 20 cm
> Side C = 5 cm   = 5 cm
>
> Multiply: V = LWH
> V = 10 cm x 20 cm x 5 cm
> V = 1 000 cu. cm
>
> | Cubic Kilometer | Cubic Hectometer | Cubic Dekameter | Cubic Meter | Cubic Decimeter | Cubic Centimeter | Cubic Millimeter |
> |---|---|---|---|---|---|---|
> | | | | | | | |
>
> Convert cubic centimeters to cubic decimeters.
>
> 1 000 cu. cm
>
> 1 .0 0 0 . = 1 cu. dm
> cu. dm   cu. cm

23

Method B
Convert all measurements to cubic decimeters (Remember Metric
Value Chart 1). Use the standard volume formula:
Volume (V) = length (L) x width (W) x height (H).
Convert calculated answer to cubic measure if needed.

Convert to like terms: Side A = 10 cm = 1 dm
                           Side B = 2 dm = 2 dm
                           Side C = 5 cm = .5 dm

Multiply: V = LWH
                           V = 1 dm x 2 dm x .5 dm
                           V = 1 cu. dm

Convert calculated   Answer is in appropriate cubic unit.
answer:

Exercise ❶ Applying Conversions

The problems that follow offer a further opportunity to use the volume formula and to
make unit conversions.

1. Determine the volume in cu. dm of the welded steel tank shown here. Convert all
   measurements to decimeters before solving the problem.

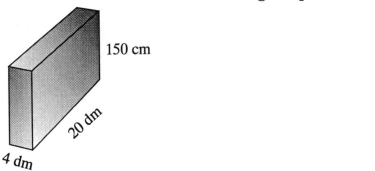

150 cm

20 dm

4 dm

_____ cu. dm

2. Convert the volume in cu. dm of the tank shown in problem #1 to cu. m. Convert
   all measurements to meters (m) before using the volume formula to help solve this
   problem.

_____ cu. m

3. A solid cube of brass has the dimensions shown. Determine the volume
   in cu. m.

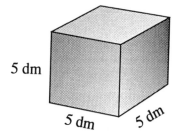

5 dm

5 dm   5 dm

_____ cu. m

24

4. Three slabs of sandstone are shown here:

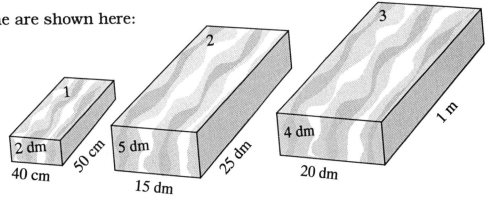

a. Determine the volume of slab #1 in cu. cm.   V = _____

b. Determine the volume of slab #2 in cu. cm.   V = _____

c. Determine the volume of slab #3 in cu. cm.   V = _____

d. Determine the total volume of slabs 1, 2, and 3 in cu. m.
                                                    V = _____

e. Determine the total volume of slabs 1, 2, and 3 in cu. dm.
                                                    V = _____

5. Ten pieces of square block are cut to the dimensions shown.
   Determine the volume as required.

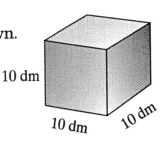

a. Determine the total volume of the ten blocks in cu. dm.   V = _____ cu. dm

b. Determine the volume of five blocks ONLY in cu. cm.   V = _____ cu. cm

c. Determine the volume of ONE block ONLY in cu. mm.   V = _____ cu. mm

25

6. A laminated piece of hardwood has the dimensions shown here. Determine the total volume in cu. cm of the 200 pieces that are in inventory.

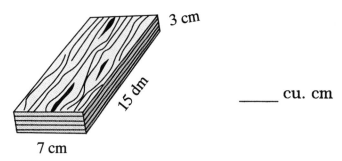

_____ cu. cm

7. Find the total of the following measurements in cu. dm. First, convert all given values to cu. dm, then add to get the total.

   2 000 cu. cm

   3 500 cu. mm

   1 500 cu. mm

   10 cu. m

   4 000 cu. mm

   5 000 cu. cm

_____ cu. dm

8. An inventory of pipe on a welding shop rack includes the pieces shown here: You will use the formula $V = \pi r^2 h$ to determine the specific volume.

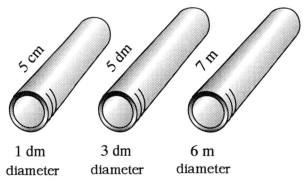

1 dm   3 dm   6 m
diameter   diameter   diameter

A = 20 pieces   B = 15 pieces   C = 12 pieces

a. Determine the total volume of all pieces of pipe A in cu. m.

V = _____

b. Determine the total volume of all pieces of pipe B in cu. m.

V = _____

c. Determine the total volume of all pieces of pipe C in cu. m .

V = _____

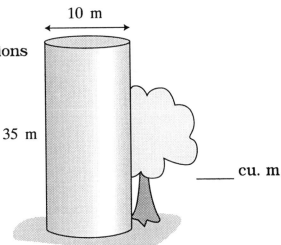

10 m

9. A concrete grain silo has the dimensions
   shown. Use the formula $V = \pi r^2 h$
   to find the volume in cu. m.

35 m

_____ cu. m

10. A flat-roofed structure has the dimensions shown. Determine the volume within
    the structure in cu. m.

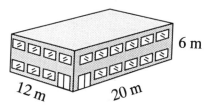

6 m

12 m   20 m

_____ cu.

11. The concrete floor slab in the structure of problem #10 is 10 cm thick. What is
    the volume of the slab of concrete in cu. m?

_____ cu. m

12. A solid cube of steel is welded to a flat plate as shown. Determine the volume as
    required.

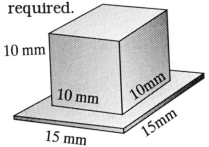

10 mm

10 mm   10mm

15 mm   15mm

a. Determine the volume of the CUBE in cu. mm.   V = _____ cu. mm

b. Determine the volume of the steel plate ONLY in cu. cm.   V = _____ cu. cm

c. Determine the volume of BOTH cube and plate in cu. dm. V = _____ cu. dm

d. ADD 2 cm to each dimension of the CUBE and determine the volume in cu mm.

V = _____ cu. mm

13. A large willow tree in our neighbor's yard was causing serious problems with their drainage system. Roots from the tree had found their way into the drain tile and it would have to be repaired or replaced. A trench for the drain tile was dug in the dimensions shown.

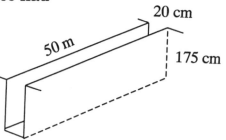

a. Determine the amount of earth removed from the trench in cu. m.

V = _____ cu. m

b. Excavation costs are $2.50 per cu. m for earth. What is the cost of excavation?

V = $_____

14. A steel plate has a cut-out as shown.

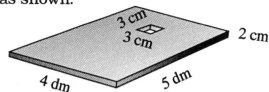

a. Determine the volume in cu. dm of the plate before the cutout was made.

V = _____ cu. dm

b. Determine the volume in cu. dm of the cut out.

V = _____ cu. dm

15. A basement is being excavated for the house shown here. The excavation is 3.5 m deep.

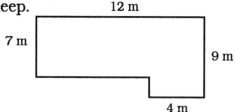

a. Determine the volume of earth to be removed, in cu. m.

V = _____ cu. m

b. The cost of excavating, using a front-end loader, is $1.50 per cu. m. What is the cost of excavation?

Cost = $_____

16. The concrete foundation wall, for the basement in problem #15, will be supported by a footing which runs under the length and width of the foundation.

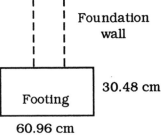

Foundation wall

Footing

30.48 cm

60.96 cm

a. How many cu. m of concrete are in the footing? (First determine the walls, but DO NOT lap the footing at the corners. Convert dimensions to meters (m) before proceeding.)

_____ cu. m

b. In English measure there are 27 cubic feet in one cubic yard. How many cubic yards does this represent?

_____ cu. yds

17. A mine shaft in the mountains of southern Colorado has an opening that measures 4 m on each of the four sides and is 120 m deep. A new ventilating system is being planned. Before ordering new air-handling equipment, the volume of air in the shaft must be determined. What is the volume of air in the shaft in cu. m?

_____ cu. m

18. A flat-bottom concrete bean storage elevator is shown.

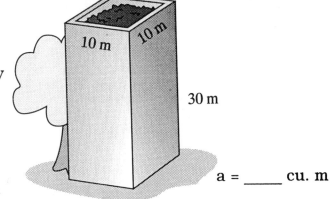

10 m

10 m

30 m

a. Determine the storage capacity when the elevator is filled to capacity in cu. m.

a = _____ cu. m

b. Determine the storage capacity in cu. dam.

b = _____ cu. dam

c. If the elevator is exactly half-full, what is the remaining capacity in cu. dm?

c = _____ cu. dm

d. Use the volume determined in Part a above. If 60% of the beans are removed, how many cu. m of beans remain?

d = _____ cu. m

e. The walls and floor of the elevator are reinforced concrete 20.32 cm thick. How many cu. m of reinforced concrete are required to construct the bean elevator? Do not lap the corners when determining the volume of concrete required.

e = _____ cu m

f. Beans can shrink as much as 5% in volume when stored over a long period of time. How many cu. m of beans does this shrinkage equal from full capacity?

f = _____ cu. m

Chapter 5

Volume Measurement-Liquid Capacity

This chapter will present examples and problems in liquid volume measure. The basic SI metric unit for liquid capacity (volume) is the **liter** (L). The standard prefixes of *kilo*, *hecto*, *deka*, *deci*, *centi*, and *milli* also apply to the liter: kiloliter (1000 liters), hectoliter (100 liters), dekaliter (10 liters), deciliter ($\frac{1}{10}$ of a liter), centiliter ($\frac{1}{100}$ of a liter), and milliliter ($\frac{1}{1000}$ of a liter).

Kiloliter	Hectoliter	Dekaliter	Liter	Deciliter	Centiliter	Milliliter

Here is a Liquid Measure Table showing simple relationships between liquid units of capacity. You will notice that conversion between simple units reflect a power of 10 —movement of the decimal ONE place. As we explore cubic lquid capacity, decimal movement is THREE places.

Liquid Measure Table

1 kiloliter (kL)	=	10 hectoliters (hL)
1 hectoliter (hL)	=	10 dekaliters (daL)
1 dekaliter (daL)	=	10 liters (L)
1 liter (L)	=	10 deciliters (dL)
1 deciliter (dL)	=	10 centiliters (cL)
1 centiliter (cL)	=	10 millimeters (mL)

As you work volume problems, you will need to move from cubic capacity based upon meters or weight based upon grams to liquid capacity based upon liters. Here is a Conversions for Liquid Capacity table to help us.

Conversions for Liquid Capacity

1 liter (L) = 1 cu. dm (1 000 cu. cm)
1 liter (L) of water weighs 1 kilogram (kg)
1 milliliter (mL) = 1 cu. cm
1 cu. cm = 1 gram (g) of water = 1 milliliter (mL)

Cubic Units   Converting to Liquid Measures

As you have learned, measurements must be in like terms to solve problems. Once like terms are established, problems involving liquid capacity have a two-step procedure: (1) determine cubic contents, and (2) convert cubic units into liquid capacity measures.

Also remember, if you must convert between cubic units, conversion involves movement of the decimal point THREE places per unit of conversion.

Example:

Find the liquid capacity of the vessel shown here. Use the standard volume formula, V = LWH.

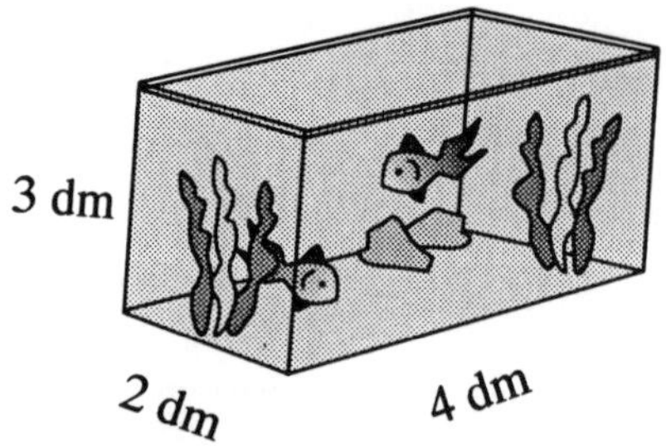

SOLUTION:

$V = L \times W \times H$

$V = 4 \text{ dm} \times 2 \text{ dm} \times 3 \text{ dm}$

$V = 4 \times 2 \times 3 = 24 \text{ cu. dm}$

$V = 24 \text{ cu. dm}$ (Now convert from cubic measure to liquid capacity)

$V = 24 \text{ liters}$ (From the conversion table, 1 cu. dm = 1 L)

NOTE: If the vessel had dimensions of L = 15 cm, W = 10 cm, and H = 12 cm, it would be advisable to convert cm to dm before working the problem.

  15 cm = 1.5 dm,
  10 cm = 1 dm
  12 cm = 1.2 dm.

  $V = LWH$
  $V = 1.5 \times 1 \times 1.2$
  $V = 1.8 \text{ cu. dm}$
  $V = 1.8 \text{ L}$ (From the conversion table, 1 L = 1 cu. dm)

Further example:

Find the liquid capacity of a cylindrical vessel that is 10 dm high with a diameter of 4 dm. Use the volume formula, $V = \pi r^2 h$.

SOLUTION:

$V = \pi r^2 h$

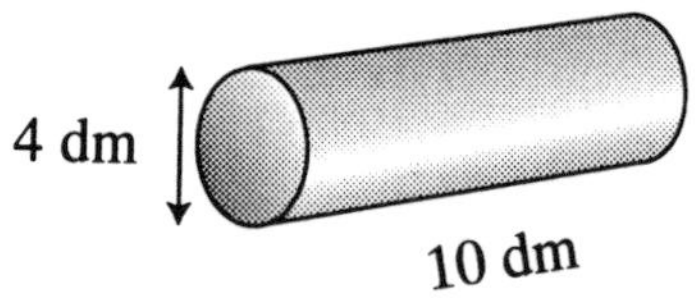

$V = 3.14 \times 2^2 \times 10$

$V = 3.14 \times 4 \times 10$

$V = 125.6 \text{ cu. dm}$

$V = 125.6 \text{ L}$

NOTE: Had this cylindrical vessel measured 75 cm high with a diameter of 25 cm, convert 75 cm to 7.5 dm and 25 cm to 2.5 dm before proceding to find the solution.

  $V = 3.14 \times 1.25^2 \times 7.5$
  $V = 3.14 \times 1.5625 \times 7.5$
  $V = 36.796875 \text{ cu. dm}$
  $V = 36.8 \text{ L}$ (Rounded)

Work the following problems. Remember! Cubic content can be converted to cubic decimeters (cu. dm) before determining the liquid measure in liters (L) OR move the decimal point THREE places to convert to liters (L).

1. An underground diesel storage tank has the dimensions shown.

3 dm   8 dm

   a. Determine the volume of the tank in cu. m.

                                        _____ cu. m

   b. How many liters (L) does the tank hold when filled to capacity?

                                          _____ L

2. A suburban city water tank has the dimensions shown.

15 dm

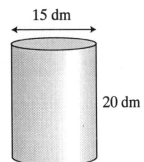

20 dm

   a. Determine the volume of the tank in cu. m.

                               _____ cu. m

   b. How many L does the tank hold when filled to capacity?

                               _____ L

3. A can of motor oil has the dimensions shown here.

8 cm

15 cm

   a. What is the volume of the can in cu. cm?

                               _____ cu. cm

   b. What is the volume of the can in cu. dm? In liters (L)?

                               _____ cu. dm

                               _____ L

   c. How many liters (L) are contained in a case of 12 cans? (Round to nearest hundredth.)

                               _____ L

d. If 3 cans of oil were removed from the case, what percentage of cans remains?

_____ %

e. Refer to Part *d* above, how many liters (L) are in the remaining cans?

_____ L

f. In a recent inventory, 17 cases of cans were counted. How many liters (L) would this equal?

_____ L

g. If the retail price for each can is $1.19, what is the total value of the inventory?

$ _____

h. If the gross profit is 40% on each can sold, how much assumed profit can be made from inventory sales?

$ _____

4. A measuring pitcher with straight sides has the dimensions shown. To find the volume use the formula: $V = \pi r^2 h$

10 cm

20 cm

a. What is the volume in cu. dm?

_____ cu. dm

b. What is the volume in cu. cm?

_____ cu. cm

c. When filled to capacity, how many liters (L) will the pitcher hold?

_____ L

d. If the pitcher is filled to $\frac{3}{4}$ capacity, how many liters (L) are in the pitcher?

_____ L

e. Water weighs 1 kilogram (kg) per liter (L). What is the weight of the water in the pitcher when filled to capacity?

_____ kg

f. Refer to Part *e* above. If 5% of the water is lost to evaporation, what is the weight of the remaining water in kg?

_____ kg

g. If 10 pitchers were each filled to $\frac{1}{2}$ capacity, how many liters (L) would that equal?

_____ L

5. A length of drainage pipe has the dimensions shown.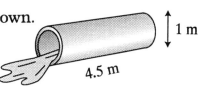

    a. How many cu. m are contained in one length of this pipe?

                                                  _____ cu. m

    b. How many liters (L) of water would one length of this pipe hold, when completely filled?

                                                  _____ L

    c. If the diameter of the pipe is changed to 0.75 m, how many cu. m would be contained in one length of this pipe?

                                                  _____ cu. m

6. Determine the volume in liters (L) of the steel tank shown here. Change all dimensions to dm before proceeding. Round to three places behind the decimal.

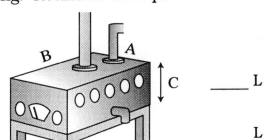

    a. A = 3 dm, B = 4 dm, C = 2 dm   _____ L

    b. A = 1 m, B = 2 m, C = 1.5 m   _____ L

    c. A = 30 cm, B = 2 dm, C = 1 m   _____ L

    d. A = 10 dm, B = 15 dm, C = 30 cm   _____ L

7. A cylindrical flat-top gasoline storage tank has the dimensions shown.

                             a. Determine the volume of the tank in cu. m.

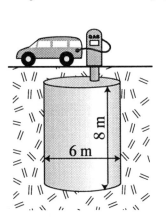

                                           _____ cu. m

                             b. Determine the volume of the tank in cu. dam.

                                         _____ cu. dam

c. Determine the volume of the tank in liters (L).

_____ L

d. If 7% of the tank's capacity was lost to evaporation, how many liters (L) would remain, assuming the tank had been filled to capacity?

_____ L

Change the diameter of the tank to 7 m and its height to 9 m.

e. What is the volume in cu. m?

_____ cu. m

f. What is the volume of the tank in liters (L)?

_____ L

g. If 30% of the tank's capacity is drained, how many liters (L) remain?

_____ L

8. A round-top gasoline tank that is mounted on a truck is shown here . Use both volume formulas to solve these problems. The diameter of the round-top is 5 dm or 2.5 dm radius. Note: The round-top is one-half of a full circle.

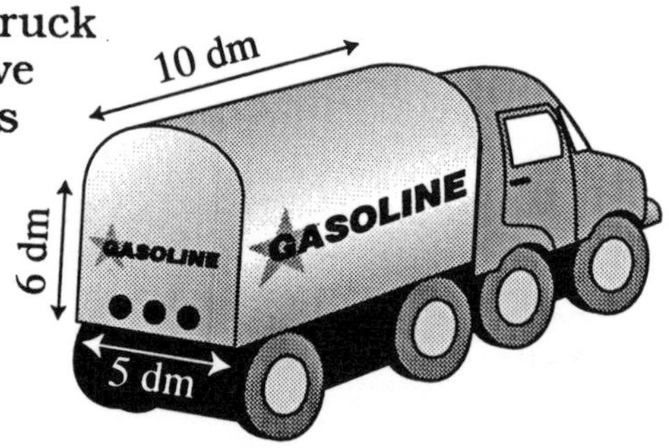

a. Determine the volume of the tank in cu. m.

_____ cu. m

b. Determine the volume of the tank in cu. dm.

_____ cu. dm

c. Determine the capacity of the tank in liters (L).

_____ L

d. If the tank was filled to the top of the straight walls ONLY, how many liters (L) are in the tank?

_____ L

e. Refer to Part c above. If 3% of the tank's capacity was lost to evaporation, how many liters (L) would remain?

_____ L

9. An open steel tank is divided into compartments as shown here.

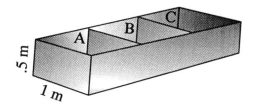

a. Compartment A is 0.5 m wide. How many cu. m are in this compartment?

_____ cu. m

b. Compartment B is 0.75 m wide. How many cu. m are in this compartment?

_____ cu. m

c. Compartment C is 1.25 m wide. How many cu. m are in this compartment?

_____ cu. m

d. How many liters (L) are in each of the 3 compartments?

A = _____ L

B = _____ L

C = _____ L

e. If the 3 compartments were each filled to 75% of their respective capacities, how many TOTAL liters (L) would be in the 3 compartments?

_____ L

10. A community swimming pool is shown here.

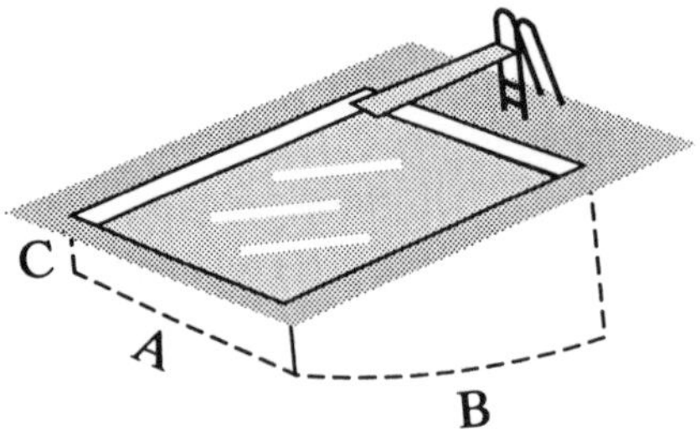

*NOTE: The average depth is 2 m.

a. Determine how many cu. m are in the pool.

_____ cu. m

b. How many liters (L) of water are needed to fill the pool to capacity?

_____ L

c. On a hot summer day, 10% of the water is lost to evaporation. How many liters (L) would this represent?

_____ L

d. ADD 5 m to the width and to the length of the pool and determine how many cu. m are in the pool based on the new size.

_____ cu. m

e. Refer to Part *d* above. How many liters (L) of water will the new, larger pool hold when filled to capacity?

_____ L

f. Determine the percent of INCREASE in capacity for the new, larger pool versus the capacity of the original pool.

_____ %

Chapter 6
Weight Measurement-Mass

This chapter will offer examples and problems in weight (mass) measurements. The relationship and decimal movement of weight measures will be very familar to you. Here is a Metric Value Chart for weight measurement.

Metric Value Chart 3 • Weight Measurement

Unit	Kilogram	Hectogram	Dekagram	Basic Unit Gram	Decigram	Centigram	Milligram
Symbol	1 kg =	1 hg =	1 dag =	1 g =	1 dg =	1 cg =	1 mg =
Base Unit Value	1000 g	100 g	10 g	1 g	0.1 g	0.01 g	0.001 g

This is the same Metric Value Chart to which you were introduced in Chapter 2. The gram merely replaces the meter. And like some length units, some weight units are more commonly used than others. The most commonly used units of weight measurement are the gram (g), the milligram (mg), and the kilogram (kg).

Movement from one weight unit to the next is by a factor of 10.

As you work weight problems, you will be asked to determine weights for objects with different metric values. These conversion facts will help you in the problem solving to follow.

Weight Measure Table

1 kilogram (kg)	=	10 hectogram (hg)
1 hectogram (hg)	=	10 dekagram (dag)
1 dekagram (dag)	=	10 gram (g)
1 gram (g)	=	10 decigram (dg)
1 decigram (dg)	=	10 centigram (cg)
1 centigram (cg)	=	10 milligram (mg)

Weight Conversions

1 cu. cm of steel	=	7.849 g
1 cu. cm of fir wood	=	.35 g
1 cu. cm of concrete	=	3 g
1 cu. cm of earth	=	2.6 g
1 cu. dm	=	1 000 cu. cm = 1 L
1 000 mL	=	1 L
1 cu. cm	=	1 mL
1 L of water	=	1 kg
1 mL or 1 cu. cm of water	=	1 g

Converting Units | Moving the Decimal

To add, subtract, multiply, or divide weight measurements, all measurements involved must be in like terms. Converting to like terms is done simply by moving the decimal point to the right or left. You can always refer to Metric Value Chart 3 to help you move between units.

Example:

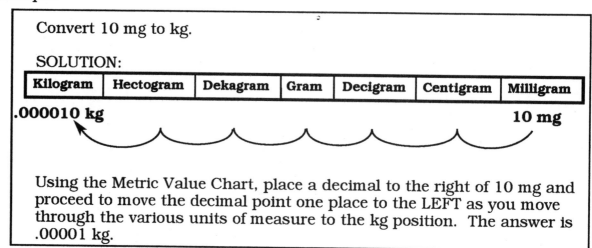

Convert 10 mg to kg.

SOLUTION:

Kilogram	Hectogram	Dekagram	Gram	Decigram	Centigram	Milligram

.000010 kg   10 mg

Using the Metric Value Chart, place a decimal to the right of 10 mg and proceed to move the decimal point one place to the LEFT as you move through the various units of measure to the kg position. The answer is .00001 kg.

Exercise 1 Converting Units

Work these problems by using the value line.

1. Change the following weights to kg:

a. 60 cg _____ kg

b. 100 g _____ kg

c. 150 dag _____ kg

d. 200 hg _____ kg

e. 700 dag _____ kg

f. 5 mg _____ kg

g. 120 dg _____ kg

h. .50 g _____ kg

i. 5.5 mg _____ kg

j. 1500 mg _____ kg

k. 25 cg _____ kg

l. Several cartons of canned goods were collected to be delivered to the needy. The cartons were: 6 cartons of peaches at 20 pounds each, 3 boxes of tomatos at 16 pounds each and 4 cartons of green beans at 18 pounds each. How many total kilograms (kg) of canned goods were delivered?
NOTE: Refer to the Conversion Chart on page 3 to convert from customary measure to metric measure.

_____ kg

Exercise ② Applying Weight Measurements

The following problems require conversions between units of measure before the actual solution process can begin. Always refer to the Metric Value Chart and the Weight Conversions Table for help.

Example:

> A piece of fir wood has these dimensions: length = 1 m, width = 1 cm, and thickness = 5 mm. Determine the weight in g.
>
> SOLUTION:
>
> First change all dimensions to cm using the Metric Value Chart. Use the formula V = LWH
>
> V = L x W x H (thickness = H)
>
> V = 100 cm x 1 cm x .5 cm = 50 cu. cm
>
> V = 50 cu. cm x .35 g = 17.5 g (.35 g = the weight of 1 cu. cm of fir wood)

1. A piece of steel bar has the dimensions shown. Use the formula V = LWH.

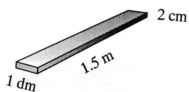
2 cm
1.5 m
1 dm

 a. Determine the weight of the steel bar in g. First convert all dimensions to cm. Then use the volume formula.

_____ g

 b. How many cu. dm are in the bar? First convert all dimensions to dm. Then use the volume formula.

_____ cu. dm

 c. Determine the weight of the steel bar in dg. Using Metric Value Chart, convert g to dg.

_____ dg

2. Concrete weighs approximately 144 pounds per cubic foot by English measure. What is the approximate weight in kg?

_____ kg

41

3. A piece of steel shafting is shown here. Use the formula $V = \pi r^2 h$.

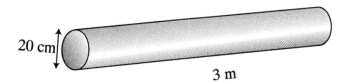

20 cm

3 m

   a. Determine the weight in kg. First, convert m to cm. Your answer in cu. cm is converted to g then to kg.

_____ kg

   b. How many cu. dm are in the shaft? First convert all dimensions to dm.

_____ cu. dm

   c. Determine the weight in g. Use the Metric Value Chart and convert kg to g.

_____ g

4. A brick wall is shown here. The weight of this brick wall is approximately 306 kg per square meter of wall surface.

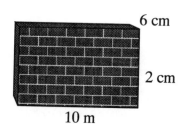

6 cm

2 cm

10 m

All measurements should be converted into meters (m) before working the following problems:

   a. What is the total weight of the wall in kg?

_____ kg

   b. How many square meters (sq. m) of wall surface does the wall contain?

_____ sq. m

   c. How many cu. m does the wall contain?

_____ cu. m

5. The swimming pool at a local apartment complex has the dimensions of 7 m wide, 12 m long with an average depth of 2 m. Determine the amount of earth excavated in cu. m, when the pool was constructed.

_____ cu. m

6. A block of steel is cut into three pieces.

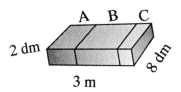

A = 1 dm wide

B = 1.5 dm wide

C = .5 dm wide

a. Determine the weight of the whole block, in kg before cutting.

_____ kg

b. Determine the weight of each block in kg.

A = _____ kg

B = _____ kg

C = _____ kg

7. The cylindrical container shown here is filled with water. Find the capacity.

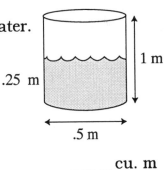

a. How many cu. m does the container hold?

_____ cu. m

b. How many liters (L) does the container hold? How many kg would this equal?

_____ L

_____ kg

c. How many liters (L) will remain in the container, when drained to the .25 m measure? Round to the nearest whole liter.

_____ L

43

8. Solve the following problems:

a. 110 kg
    - 20 g
    ────────

b. 300 hg
    - 50 dag
    ────────

a = _____ kg
b = _____ hg

c. 200 kg
    - 50 hg
    ────────

d. 10 g
    + 1.5 dg
    ────────

c = _____ kg
d = _____ g

9. A steel container has the dimensions shown here:

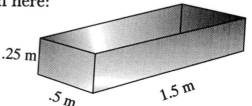

.25 m   .5 m   1.5 m

a. When filled to capacity, determine the weight of the water in kg.

_____ kg

b. How many cu. dm of water will the container hold when filled to capacity?

_____ cu. dm

c. When filled to capacity, determine the weight of the water in g.

_____ g

10. A circular steel shim used for leveling machinery is shown:

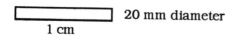 20 mm diameter
1 cm

a. Determine the weight to the nearest hundredth of 500 shims in kg.

_____ kg

11. A regular building brick is shown. Each brick weighs approximately 84 grams (g).

   a. What is the weight of 1000 brick, in kg?

   _____ kg

   b. What is the weight of 500 brick, in g.

   _____ g

12. A cylindrical concrete grain storage elevator (silo) is shown here. The sloping base reduces the capacity by 5%.

   Note: 1 bushel of wheat = 1.25 cu. ft.
   1 bushel of wheat = 0.0354 cu. m
   1 bushel of wheat = 60 lbs. wgt.
   1 bushel of wheat = 27.2 kg
   1 bushel of wheat = 35.4 L

   10 m

   35 m

   a. What is the net capacity in cu. m?

   _____ cu. m

   b. What is the net capacity in bushels of wheat?

   _____ bu.

   c. If 3% of the full silo were emptied, how many bushels of wheat remain?

   _____ bu.

   d. What is the net weight of the wheat in kg when the silo is filled to capacity?

   _____ kg

   e. How many liters (L) of wheat are in the silo when filled to capacity?

   _____ L

   f. How many liters (L) are left in the silo if 15% of the contents are removed?

   _____ L

Chapter 7
Temperature Measurement

This chapter will explore both Celsius and Fahrenheit standards of measure for temperature. The English unit of measure is the Fahrenheit (F) scale, named after Gabriel Fahrenheit, the inventor of the mercury thermometer. The SI Metric unit of measure is the Celsius (C) scale (sometimes referred to as the Centigrade scale), named after its creator Anders Celsius.

Compare the Celsius and Fahrenheit thermometers shown here. Common temperatures are noted to aid in comparisons.

On the Fahrenheit thermometer, water freezes at 32°F and boils at 212°F. You will notice that water freezes at 0°C and boils at 100°C on the Celsius thermometer.

To solve many problems presented in this chapter, formulas are required. Here are some sample problems to get you started.

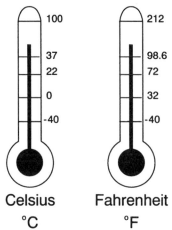

Celsius
°C

Fahrenheit
°F

Examples:

•To find degrees Celsius (C) when the Fahrenheit (F) temperature is known, use the formula:

$$C = \frac{5(°F-32°)}{9}$$

Convert 80°F to °C

$C = \frac{5(80°-32°)}{9}$ (Substitute in formula)

$C = \frac{5 \cdot 48}{9}$ (Work within parenthesis first)

$C = \frac{240}{9}$

$C = 26.7°F$

•To find degrees Fahrenheit (F) when the Celsius (C) temperature is known, use the formula:

$$F = 32 + \left(\frac{9}{5}°C\right)$$

Convert 26.7°C to °F .

$$F = 32° + \left(\frac{9}{5}°C\right)$$

$$F = 32° + \left(\frac{9 \cdot 26.7°}{5}\right)$$

$$F = 32° + 48.06°$$

$$F = 80.06°F \text{ or } 80°F$$

Exercise 1 — Temperature Measurements

1. The following temperatures were recorded on successive days in an auto repair shop.

Monday	28°C
Tuesday	30°C
Wednesday	26°C
Thursday	32°C
Friday	29°C
Saturday	28°C
Sunday	30°C

What is the average temperature in degrees Celsius? (To find the average temperature, ADD all daily temperature readings and divide by the number of days.)

_____ °C

2. Compare the two thermometers shown on page 45 and estimate the approximate temperature in degrees Celsius (C) for the Fahrenheit (F) temperature shown.

a. 50°F   a = _____ °C

b. 75°F   b = _____ °C

c. 150°F   c = _____ °C

d. 27°F   d = _____ °C

e. 175°F   e = _____ °C

f. 65°F   f = _____ °C

g. 15°F   g = _____ °C

h. 212°F   h = _____ °C

i. 90°F   i = _____ °C

j. 100°F   j = _____ °C

k. 37°F   k = _____ °C

3. An air conditioning system is installed in the shop and reduces the temperature by 20%. Determine each of the daily readings for the shop when the air conditioner is operating Monday through Sunday. Use 20% as the estimated temperature reduction. (The answer will be 20% less than the temperature shown for that specific day before air conditioning was installed.) During the hot summer months it is common practice to keep air conditioning systems operating every day of the week including non-work days, Saturday and Sunday. It would be too expensive to shut down an air conditioning system after work on Friday and then start up again on Monday morning.

To find the average temperature, multiply the original average daily temperature by 20% (.20) and SUBTRACT this amount to reach the average daily temperature with the air conditioning system in operation.

a. Monday $\qquad$ a = _____ °C

b. Tuesday $\qquad$ b = _____ °C

c. Wednesday $\qquad$ c = _____ °C

d. Thursday $\qquad$ d = _____ °C

e. Friday $\qquad$ e = _____ °C

f. Saturday $\qquad$ f = _____ °C

g. Sunday $\qquad$ g = _____ °C

h. Determine the average temperature Monday through Sunday.

h = _____ °C

4. Determine the oven temperature in degrees Celsius (C) for the Fahrenheit (F) temperature given. Round off your answer to the nearest whole number.

Use the formula: $C = \dfrac{5(°F - 32°)}{9}$.

a. 300°F $\qquad$ a = _____ °C

b. 325°F $\qquad$ b = _____ °C

c. 350°F $\qquad$ c = _____ °C

d. 275°F $\qquad$ d = _____ °C

e. 250°F $\qquad$ e = _____ °C

f. 225°F $\qquad$ f = _____ °C

5. 72°F is considered a comfortable room temperature. What is the comparable temperature in degrees Celsius?

_____ °C

6. 98.6°F is the normal body temperature. What is the comparable temperature in degrees Celsius?

_____ °C

7. A certain automobile radiator thermostat is set to begin opening at 180°F water temperature. What is the comparable water temperature in degrees Celsius?

_____ °C

8. Elena has a slight fever and will not be able to go on her Girl Scout picnic today. Her fever is 101°F. What is her comparable fever in degrees Celsius?

_____ °C

9. In the southwest desert region of the U.S. a record high temperature of 122°F was recorded last summer. What is the comparable temperature in degrees Celsius?

_____ °C

10. Two pieces of steel bar were welded together to form a "T" as shown. The fillet weld was made at a temperature of 1600°C .

The weld cools to a handling temperature of 20°C in about 30 minutes. Determine the cooling rate for this weld in degrees Celsius per minute. The cooling rate is the temperature drop of an object divided by the time it takes for the temperature to drop.

Develop a formula in this manner:

Use the temperature of the weld less handling temperature divided by the time it takes for the temperature to drop. The formula would be as follows:

$\frac{1600° - 20°}{30}$ = Cooling rate/minute. Round to the nearest tenth.

_____ °C /minute

11. Change the temperature of the weld to 1450°C. The handling temperature and cooling time remain unchanged. Find the cooling rate per minute. Round to the nearest tenth.

_____ °C / minute

12. "Summertime and the living is easy." is a line from a well known song. But not always. Sometimes summertime storms can change the outlook very quickly. A recent storm enveloped our town and the temperature dropped from 90°F to 65°F in less than 30 minutes. What did the drop in temperature represent in degrees Celsius? Round to the nearest tenth.

_____ °C

13. A new sidewalk was just poured at our school. At a temperature of 32°C the concrete dries at a rate of 6 mm thickness per hour. A rise in temperature of 5°C increases the drying time by 1 hour. The thickness of the sidewalk is 150 mm.

a. Using the above figures, how long will it take the concrete to dry, at 32°C?

_____ hours

b. At a temperature rise to 42°C, how much longer will it take the concrete to dry?

_____ hours

c. At a temperature rise to 52°C, how much longer will it take the concrete to dry?

_____ hours

d. At a temperature rise to 57°C, how much longer will it take the concrete to dry?

_____ hours

14. Convert these oven temperatures using the proper formulas for converting between the units of measure. Be accurate to tenths of degrees.

a. 260°F   _____ °C
b. 310°F   _____ °C
c. 180°C   _____ °F
d. 410°F   _____ °C
e. 220°C   _____ °F
f. 160°C   _____ °F
g. 225°F   _____ °C
h. 475°F   _____ °C
i. 230°C   _____ °F
j. 155°C   _____ °F
k. 190°C   _____ °F
l. 425°F   _____ °C
m. 390°F   _____ °C
n. 170°C   _____ °F
o. 145°C   _____ °F

15. On a recent fishing trip to the lake, the temperature rose from 72°F to 90°F in just over an hour. How many degrees Celsius did the rise in temperature represent?

_____ °C

16. One day last winter while ice fishing at Gun Lake, the temperature dropped from 40°F to 25°F in 2 hours. How many degrees Celsius did the drop in temperature represent? Carry the decimal one place.

_____ °C

17. In our area, winter storms can also be unpredictable. Last winter we experienced a rise in temperature from 50°F to 70°F in about 3 hours, on a sunny January afternoon. What did the rise in temperature represent in degrees Celsius?

_____ °C

Chapter 8
Metrics & Percents

This chapter will present examples and problems covering percentages. The purpose is to explore three methods used to solve percentage problems. Percentage problems can often be confusing. Our mission is to take away the "mystery" by thoroughly explaining the solution process involved in solving percentage problems.

The Business Method and the Algebraic Method are the most widely used, but a lesser used third method, the Direct Ratio Method, will also be explained in this chapter. You will have the opportunity to become familiar with all methods so that you can decide which best suits you. In the "work world," often any method can be used to reach the solution to a percentage problem.

Most percentage problems concern a portion of money or numbers. To be effective in solving percentage problems it will be necessary, first, to develop problem solving skills through study and instruction, and, then, put those skills to use. Spend time and effort becoming familiar with the formulas presented in this chapter and how to use them.

Problems will be offered using both English and metric systems of measure. The formulas REMAIN THE SAME, whether using English or SI metric measure.

Converting Decimals & Fractions to Percents

Examine these conversions:

Decimal FROM ⟶	Percent TO	Fraction FROM ⟶	Percent TO
a .931	93.1%	e. $\frac{8}{8}$	100%
b. .19	19%	f. $\frac{5}{20}$	25%
c. 1.50	150%	g. $\frac{3}{4}$	75%
d. .005	.5%	h. $\frac{65}{100}$	65%

Let's explain these conversions.

Decimal to Percent
a. With .931, move the decimal point TWO places to the right and add a % sign (93.1%).

b. With .19, move the decimal point TWO places to the right and add a % sign (19%). Now remove the decimal point because there are no digits to the right.

c. With 1.50, move the decimal point TWO places to the right and add a % sign (150%).

d. With .005, move the decimal point TWO places to the right and add a % sign after the 5 (.5%).

REMEMBER! When converting between decimals and percents the movement of the decimal point is ALWAYS TWO PLACES.

Fraction to Percent

e. $\frac{8}{8}$ = 1 or 100%

f. $\frac{5}{20}$ = $\frac{1}{4}$ or 25% Divide the numerator (1) by the denominator (2), add a % sign.

g. $\frac{3}{4}$ = 75% Divide the numerator (3) by the denominator (4), add a % sign.

h. $\frac{65}{100}$ = $\begin{cases} .65 = 65\% \\ \quad \text{or} \\ \frac{\text{numerator}}{\text{denominator}} \text{ plus a \% sign.} \end{cases}$

Exercise ◀1▶ Decimals & Fractions to Percents

Use your new skills to complete this table:

Decimal		Percent
.741	=	_____
.29	=	_____
_____	=	125%
_____	=	1%

Fraction		Percent
4/4	=	_____
4/20	=	_____
_____	=	25%
_____	=	55%

54

Method 1   The Business Method: Part, Rate & Base

The Business Method concerns itself with the varying relationships of part, rate and base.

We can use this simple graphic to help us understand these relationships.

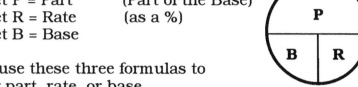

Let P = Part   (Part of the Base)
Let R = Rate   (as a %)
Let B = Base

We can use these three formulas to solve for part, rate, or base.

$$P = RB \qquad R = \frac{P}{B} \qquad B = \frac{P}{R}$$

Finding the PART

To discover which formula to use, place your finger over the P for Part. Notice that R & B are left side by side. The formula becomes P = RB or Part = Rate x Base.

Example:

Find the Part when Rate = 10% and Base = 50.

SOLUTION:

Use the formula P = RB.

P = .10 x 50 = 5
P = 5 (5 is 10% of 50)

Finding the RATE

To discover which formula to use, place your finger over R for Rate and notice the P is over B. The formula becomes R = Part divided by Base.

Example:

Find the Rate when Part = 5 and Base = 50.

SOLUTION:

Use the formula $R = \frac{P}{B}$.

R = 5 ÷ 50 = .1
R = .1 or 10%

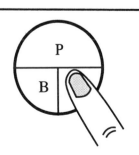

Finding the BASE

To discover which formula to use, place your finger over the B for Base and notice that P is over R. The formula becomes B = Part divided by Rate.

Example:

Find the Base when Part = 5 and Rate = 10% (.10)

SOLUTION:

Use the formula B = $\frac{P}{R}$

B = 5 ÷10% (.10)
B = 50

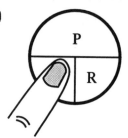

Method 2   The Algebraic Method: Ratio & Proportion

Let's move on and learn about the Algebraic Method. Don't let the word *algebra* concern you! You were actually using a form of algebra when you used the three business formulas. In each of the three formulas, you found the value of the unknown and that's a form of algebra. When using the Algebraic Method to solve for an unknown (*X* will stand for the "unknown"), we will be using another form of algebra known as "ratio and proportion."

Finding the PART

Example:

Find the Part, when: X = Part
                       50 = Base
                   10% = Rate

SOLUTION:

Set up a ratio: X : 50 :: 10 : 100   (X is to Base 50 as 10% is to 100%)
This ratio sets up a comparison only.

Now set the proportion. (The second number in the ratio ALWAYS becomes the denominator in the proportion.)

The proportion is: $\frac{X}{50} = \frac{10}{100}$

Cross multiply: $\frac{X}{50} \diagup\!\!\!\!\diagdown \frac{10}{100}$

$$100X = 500$$

Divide both sides by 100: $\frac{100x}{100} = \frac{500}{100}$

100X divided by 100 leaves X alone on one side. 500 divided by 100 leaves 5 on the other side.

Therefore X = 5 (part)

To prove the proportion, substitute 5 for X in the original equation.

$\frac{5}{50}$ = $\frac{10}{100}$ and cross multiply to get $\frac{500}{500}$.

The proportion is TRUE because BOTH sides are equal.

Finding the RATE

Example:

Find the RATE, when: 5 = Part
                                   50 = Base
                                     X = Rate

SOLUTION:

Set up a ratio: 5 : 50 :: X : 100   (50 is to 5 as X is to 100%)
This ratio sets up a comparison only.

The proportion is: $\frac{5}{50}$ = $\frac{X}{100}$

Cross multiply: $\frac{5}{50}$ $\frac{X}{100}$

                50X = 500

Divide both sides by 50: $\frac{50x}{50}$ = $\frac{500}{50}$

50X divided by 50 leaves X alone on one side and 500 divided by 50 leaves 10 alone on the other side.

The rate equals 10 or 10%.

Prove the proportion!

Finding the BASE

Example:

Find the BASE, when: 5 = Part
                                   X = Base
                              10% = Rate

SOLUTION:

Set up a ratio: 5 : X :: 10 : 100   (5 is to X as 10% is to 100%)
This ratio sets up a comparison only.

The Proportion is: $\frac{10}{100} = \frac{5}{X}$

Cross multiply: $\frac{10}{100} \times \frac{5}{X}$

$$10X = 500$$

Divide both sides by 10: $\frac{10x}{10} = \frac{500}{10}$

10X divided by 10 leaves X alone on one side and 500 divided by 10 leaves 50 alone on the other side

The base equals 50.

Prove the proportion!

Stay with the rules when using algebra to solve ratio and proportion problems. No short cuts please!

Method 3 The Direct Ratio Method

Let's move on to the Direct Ratio Method and learn what it's all about. This method is the least understood and used. In some ways it's the easiest method when applicable.

In this method we compare two numbers, such as 1 and 4. We place the 1 over 4 to form a fraction $\frac{1}{4}$ (or ratio). In this ratio, 1 is $\frac{1}{4}$ the value of 4 , and 4 is 4 times the value of 1.

Be Cautious. It is essential to have a sound working knowledge of fractions and decimals to use direct ratio properly.

Example:

What percentage of unproductive land would 8 acres be of an 80 acre farm?

SOLUTION:

Think 8 acres is to 80 acres and set the ratio:

$8 : 80 = \frac{8}{80} = \frac{1}{10} = .10 = 10\%$ of unproductive land.

After the fraction is formed it must be converted to its decimal equivalent and finally to a percent. The fraction $\frac{8}{80}$ was simplified to $\frac{1}{10}$ and then converted to the decimal .10   (1 divided by 10 = .1 or .10)   .10 =10%.

58

> Prove the answer by multiplying 80 acres by 10% (.10) to get 8 or 8 acres. Working back through the problem, you can prove the Base (80 acres) by dividing 8 by 10% or .10 to get 80 or 80 acres.

Be careful when using this method!

Now, after using all three methods to solve percentage problems you may have decided on a method which best suits you. The advantage is that when working these types of problems YOU have a choice of which method to use.

Exercise ➋ Solving Percentage Problems

Solve these problems by using YOUR method.

1. 15 is _____ % of 75?

2. 20% of 75 = _____

3. 15 is 25% of _____

4. A worker received a base rate of $12.00 per hour. She received a production bonus of $2.00 per hour for her work this week. What percent (to the nearest tenth percent) of her base pay did the bonus represent? (Find the rate.)

_____ %

5. The Smith family saves 10% of its monthly gross income of $1,600.00. How much do they save? (Find the part.)

$ _____

6. Central Diesel Service showed a profit of $1,715 on service charges of $7950. What percent was the profit (to the nearest tenth percent) on service charges? (Find the rate.)

_____ %

7. Uptown Auto Service showed a 12% profit on service charges of $9,050. How much profit did they make?

$ _____

8. A house is insured for 80% of its value. The insurance coverage is $50,000. What is the value of the house?

$ _____

9. A carnation grower had some problems with her heating system last month and lost 75 plants due to the low temperature. Before the loss she had 650 plants. What was the percentage of loss?

_____ %

10. Refer to problem #9 above. If the growers investment was $0.75 per plant, how much money did she lose?

$ _____

The following problems will involve a variety of solutions to metric related problems. Remember, the formulas remain the same!

11. A concrete finisher poured and finished 80 square meters (sq. m) of concrete on Monday. On Tuesday, he completed 90 sq. m. What is the percentage of additional work completed on Tuesday? (Try ratio and proportion for this problem.) 90 : 100 :: 10 : X (10 = 10 sq. m increase)

_____ %

12. A concrete finisher completed 100 sq. m of concrete on Thursday and increased this total by 20% on Friday. How many sq. m of concrete did he finish on Friday?

_____ sq. m

13. A garden plot measures 6 m x 12 m in size. What is the area in sq. m?

_____ sq. m

14. Refer to problem #13 above. The gardener will plant 20% of the area in green beans and 15% of the area in corn. How many sq. m will be planted in green beans and corn?

green beans = _____ sq. m

corn = _____ . sq. m

15. A landscape contractor is preparing an 80 acre site for sod production. (There are 43,560 square feet in one acre.) Approximately how many square meters (sq. m) does this represent? (Refer to the Conversion Chart in Chapter 1)

_____ sq. m

16. Refer to problem #15 above. Before planting, the entire acreage is prepared with enriched topsoil to a depth of 15 cm (approx. 6"). Approximately how many cubic meters of top soil are required?

_____ cu. m

17. Refer to problem #16 above. If 10% of the topsoil is actually fertilizer, how many cu. m of fertilizer are used?

_____ cu m

18. A machinist mills a piece of material that is 10 cm wide, 25 cm long and 5 cm thick. It is milled to a thickness of 4 cm. What percentage of material is wasted in the milling process? (Note, the length and width of the piece of material has no bearing on the solution.) You might consider using the DIRECT RATIO method to find the solution.

Think this problem through very carefully. Consider that 1 cm wasted is to 5 cm or 1:5. Form the fraction and convert to a decimal then to a percent.

_____ %

19. Refer to problem #18 above. Change the thickness of the material to 4 cm before milling. Mill to a depth of 3 cm and determine the percent of waste. Use ratio and proportion to solve this problem. I'll help you get started. First set the ratio, 4 cm : 100% :: 1 cm : X or 4 : 100 :: 1 : X. Now set the proportion and proceed.

_____ %

20. Bob is 6'2" tall. How many meters (m) tall is Bob? Refer to the Conversion Chart in Chapter 1.

_____ m

21. Refer to problem #20 above. Jim is 98% of Bob's height. How many meters (m) tall is Jim? Find the Part using the Business Method.

_____ m

22. Frank is away from home a total of 8 hours on a school day. Classes account for 7 hours and lunch accounts for 30 minutes. What percentage of the school day is used for commuting to and from school? Use ratio and proportion to solve this problem.

_____ %

23. George lives 2 km from school and David lives 1.5 km from school. What percentage LESS distance does David live?

_____ %

24. There are 700 bolts, each 2 cm long, in inventory at the Acme Wire Works. There are also 550 bolts which are 3 cm long. What percentage MORE of 2 cm bolts are in inventory?

_____ %

25. A steel tube is 12 cm long. An aluminum tube is 25% longer. How long is the aluminum tube?

_____ cm

26. A piece of aluminum tubing is 1.5 m long. Approximately how many inches long would this represent in customary measure?

_____ "

27. A 10K (km) race is being run next Saturday around South Lake at Washington Park. Approximately how many miles would this represent in customary measure?

_____ miles

28. My cousin Chuck weighs approximately 68 kg. I weigh about 15% more. What is my weight in pounds?

_____ lbs.

29. Refer to problem #28 above. My cousin Marge, weighs 25% less than I do. How much does Marge weigh in kg?

_____ kg

30. A 100-yard race covers approximately how many km?

_____ km

In this chapter, you have solved many different types of percentage problems. The wide variety of problems were offered to help you develop skills in solving problems using different methods. Why do we spend this much time developing these skills? Because percentage related problems are with us almost everyday of our lives! Congratulations on your achievement!

Chapter 9
Combination Problems

Problems of every variety are offered in this chapter, providing you the opportunity to use many different conversions and formulas. Most metric measures will be represented. All measurements should be in like terms before proceeding to find solutions.

You may need to review past chapters before you proceed. As always, accuracy is important, therefore be patient with yourself as you master this chapter.

Exercise ❶ Putting It All Together   part #3

1. A steel bar is shown here. It has been divided into three unequal parts.

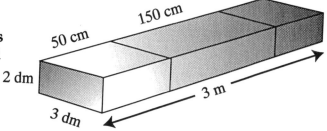

   a. Determine the length of part #3 in cm.

   _____ cm

   b. Determine the weight of the entire bar in kg.

   _____ kg

2. Gussets are cut from a piece of plywood as shown.

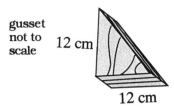

gusset not to scale 12 cm

12 cm

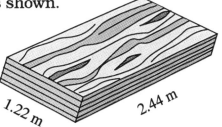

1.22 m   2.44 m

   a. How many square meters (m) are in the sheet of plywood?
      (Round the decimal to three places.)

   _____ sq. m

   b. Disregard cutting loss and determine how many <u>whole</u> gussets can be cut from the piece of plywood. (Think this through.)

   _____

65

c. How many square centimeters are in each gusset?

_____ sq. cm

d. How many square centimeters of uncut plywood are left?

_____ sq. cm

3. A circular cutout is removed from a piece of aluminum sheeting as shown here.

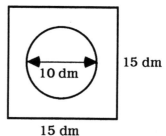

a. What is the area of the sheet in square decimeters (dm) before the cutout was made?

_____ sq. dm

b. What is the area of the circular cutout in sq. dm?

_____ sq. dm

4. Determine the area of the gussets shown here.

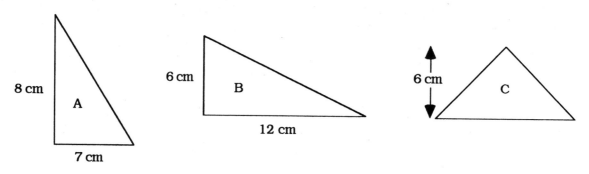

A = _____ sq. cm   B = _____ sq. dm   C = _____ sq. mm

5. Emily's dog, Sadie enjoys playing Frisbie. One time she jumped almost 8 feet in the air to catch a Frisbie. How many meters (m) would that equal?

_____ m

6. Solve the following:

a. 9 mm + 5 cm + 12 dm = _____ m

b. 10 m - 15 cm = _____ dm

c. 4 m - 4 cm = _____ cm

d. 5 kg - 10 hg = _____ g

e. 10 dm x 15 cm = _____ dm

f. 15 cm - 50 mm = _____ mm

g. 25 dm x 5 m = _____ cm

h. 95 cm + 10 mm = _____ cm

i. 15 mg + 10 cg = _____ mg

j. 100 mg - 5 cg = _____ cg

k. 9 cm + 5 mm = _____ dm

l. 15 hm + 5 m = _____ m

m. 1.5 m x 4 cm = _____ dm

n. 5 mL + 10 dL + 2 kL = _____ L

o. 15 mm + 10 cm + 5 dm = _____ dm

7. A flat metal plate is cut and drilled to the dimensions shown here.

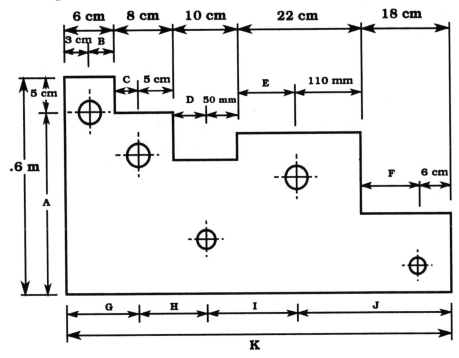

Determine the following dimensions, in cm.

A = _____ cm   B = _____ cm   C = _____ cm   D = _____ cm

E = _____ cm   F = _____ cm   G = _____ cm   H = _____ cm

I = _____ cm   J = _____ cm   K = _____ cm

8. A piece of sheet metal is rolled to form the pipe as shown here.

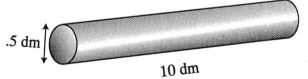

.5 dm

10 dm

   a. Determine the volume of the pipe in cu. dm.

_____ cu. dm

   b. What is the width of the sheet in dm before rolling? Use the formula C = πd for circumference which equals the width.

_____ dm

9. A metal tank is constructed to the dimensions shown.

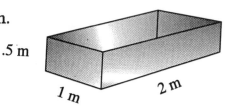

.5 m

1 m

2 m

   a. Determine the volume of the tank in cu. m.

_____ cu. m

   b. When completely filled with water, determine the weight of the water in kg.

_____ kg

10. A piece of pine lumber is shown here.
     It is cut to the dimensions noted.

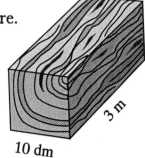

10 dm

3 m

10 dm

   a. What is the volume of the piece of lumber in cu. dm?

_____ cu. dm

   b. How many pieces, 10 dm wide, 25 cm thick and 1.5 m long, can be cut from the piece? (Disregard waste from cutting.)

_____

11. Change 5 sq. km to the following units:

a. _____ sq. hm   b. _____ sq. dam   c. _____ sq. m

d. _____ sq. dm   c. _____ sq. cm

12. Solve the following distance, rate and time problems:

a. If a car travels at a constant speed of 80 km per hour, how many km are traveled in 2 hours and 30 minutes? Use ratio and proportion to solve this problem.

_____ km

b. If a car is driven at an average speed of 90 km per hour, how much time will it take to travel 405 km? (Show the time in hours and minutes.) Use Direct Ratio to solve this problem.

_____ hours _____ minutes

c. What average speed in km per hour must a car maintain to cover a distance of 350 km in 5 hours? Use Direct Ratio to solve this problem.

_____ km per hour

d. A race car is driven at an average speed of 150 km per hour. Approximately how long will it take to travel 10 km? Use ratio and proportion to solve this problem.

_____ minutes

13. Mary had a recipe that called for 2 cups of milk. In English measure that would equal 1 pint or 16 ounces. How many grams (g) would that equal in metric measure? (Consult Appendix A for conversions.)

_____ g

14. Mary's recipe also calls for 3 tablespoons (T) of butter. How many mL would that equal? (Consult Appendix A for conversions.)

_____ mL

15. Mary was somewhat confused because the oven temperature was to be set at 165 degrees Celsius (C). The oven temperature on her range was only shown in degrees Fahrenheit (F). At about what Fahrenheit (F) temperature would she set the thermostat on her range?

_____ °F

16. Mary measures 5'3" tall or 63" or about 157.5 cm or about 1.575 m. She is 3 inches taller than her friend, Julie. How tall is Julie in cm?

_____ cm

17. Mary weighs 110 pounds or about 49.5 kg. She weighs 10 pounds more than Julie. How many kg does Julie weigh?

_____ kg

18. The track at our school stadium is 400 meters (m) long. How many feet in English measure would that equal?

_____ feet

19. The average city block in our town is 600 feet long and 300 feet wide. Convert these measurements to meters (m)

_____ meters long

_____ meters wide

20. Jane enjoys jogging around her end of town at least three times each week. She usually covers a distance equal to 10 blocks long and 2 blocks wide each time she jogs. How many meters (m) does that equal?

_____ m

21. Elena is on the school track team. She can high-jump 6'3". Her goal is to reach 6'6" this year. How many meters would that equal?

_____ m

Chapter 10
Metrics & Technology

This chapter offers a variety of problems which relate to technology. In this chapter you will have an opportunity to use your skills in algebra, geometry, and trigonometry to solve problems.

Right-angle Trigonometry Using a Calculator

A calculator is a fine tool to help solve widely varying mathematical problems. This section has been included to develop your calculator skills with right-angle trigonometry. You will be using common functions to solve for unknown angles and sides.

Finding an unknown angle.

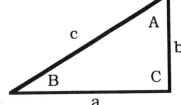

Function	Given	To find B	To find A
Sin ∠	$= \dfrac{\text{Side Opposite}}{\text{Hypotenuse}}$	$\text{Sin } B = \dfrac{b}{c}$	$\text{Sin } A = \dfrac{a}{c}$
Cos ∠	$= \dfrac{\text{Side Adjacent}}{\text{Hypotenuse}}$	$\text{Cos } B = \dfrac{a}{c}$	$\text{Cos } A = \dfrac{b}{c}$
Tan ∠	$= \dfrac{\text{Side Opposite}}{\text{Side Adjacent}}$	$\text{Tan } B = \dfrac{b}{a}$	$\text{Tan } A = \dfrac{a}{b}$

Finding an unknown side.

Side b = Sin B x c	**Side a** = Sin A x c	**Side c** = b ÷ Sin B
Cos A x c	Cos B x c	a ÷ Cos B
Tan B x a	Tan A x b	a ÷ Sin A
		b ÷ Cos A

Trigonometry functions are easily determined with the use of a scientific calculator where angle functions are designated to the power:

$$\boxed{\text{Sin}^{-1}}, \boxed{\text{Cos}^{-1}}, \boxed{\text{Tan}^{-1}}.$$

Example:

Find angle B when b = 8 and c = 14.

SOLUTION:

Use the formula $\text{Sin } B = \dfrac{b}{c}\left(\dfrac{\text{side opposite}}{\text{hypotenuse}}\right)$.

$\text{Sin } B = \dfrac{8}{14}$
$\text{Sin } B = .57142$
$B = 34\ 50\ 57.5$ or rounded 34°51'

Operation: Put .57142 into your calculator and press $\boxed{\text{Sin}^{-1}}$ key to get 34.849306, now press $\boxed{\circ\ \cdots}$ key to get 34° 50'57.5", round your answer to 34° 51'.

Example:

Find side b when B = 60° and a = 10.

SOLUTION:

Use the formula b = TAN B x a
b = 1.7320 x 10
b = 17.32

Operation: Put 60 into your calculator and press tan key to get 1.7320, multiply by 10 to get 17.3205, round to 17.32 for side b.

Therefore: To find the length of a side, use the $\boxed{\text{Sin}}$, $\boxed{\text{Cos}}$, or $\boxed{\text{Tan}}$ key for the angle in the problem and apply the appropriate formula. To find the angle press the $\boxed{\text{Sin}^{-1}}$, $\boxed{\text{Cos}^{-1}}$, $\boxed{\text{Tan}^{-1}}$ key, then press the $\boxed{\circ\ \cdots}$ key for degree of angle.

Exercise 1 Problem Solving: Metrics & Technology

The problems that follow require knowledge of algebra, geometry and trigonometry. You are encouraged to use your calculator, especially for the trigonomety problems.

1. Find A if b = 8 and c = 14.

A = ____

2. Find side b if B = 35° and c =14.

Side b = _____

3. Find side a if B = 35° and c = 14.

Side a = _____

4. Find side c if B = 35° and b = 8.

Side c = _____

5. Complete this chart for angles and values. Use your calculator. For angles, round up your answer to degrees and minutes.

FUNCTION	ANGLE	VALUE
a. Sine	37°	______
b. Cosine	31°	______
c. Tangent	51°	______
d. Sine	______	0.5150
e. Tangent	______	0.6494
f. Cosine	______	0.9962

6. A county road bridge is 8 meters (m) wide and 18 meters (m) long. What is the area of the bridge deck in square meters?

sq. m = _____

7. A new entrance ramp to the interstate highway east of town is 212.8 m long and rises 9.12 m. What is the degree of rise?

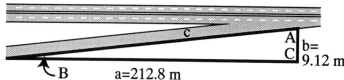

B = ____

8. Refer to problem #7 above. The ramp is 12.15 m wide. How many cubic meters (cu. m) of earth fill are required? Round to the nearest full cubic meter.

Cubic Meters ____

9. A drafter is preparing a drawing for a machine shop. The shop will use the pattern to cut steel plating. Find the missing values.

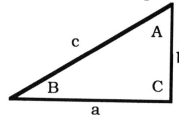

C = 90°
b = 9 "
a = 12"

Find: ∠B

∠A

Side c

B = ____

A = ____

c = ____

NOTE: Work the following problems with paper and pencil. Use your calculator when necessary.

10. A technician is preparing an estimate for a production run of tubing shown here. How many square centimeters of plate will be required to produce 150 tubes? Round your answer to the next whole number.

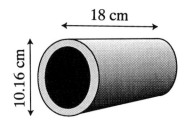

____ sq. cm

74

11. A surveyor is completing the survey of a piece of mountain property shown here.

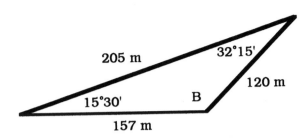

a. Find the missing angle B.

∠B = _____

b. What is the perimeter of the property?

P = _____

12. What is the perimeter and area of this metal machine base?

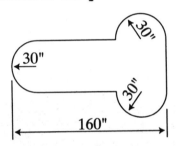

Note: 30" = 76.2 cm
      160" = 406.4 cm

P = _____ cm

A = _____ sq. cm

13. A certain popular sedan has a V/6 cylinder engine. Each piston has a diameter (d) of 8.89 cm (3.5") and a stroke (h) of 7.62 cm. (3"). Determine the piston displacement for this engine in liters (L). (Refer to chapter 5 if needed.)

HINT: Use the appropriate formula for volume where h equals stroke. FIRST convert centimeter (cm) measurements to decimeter (dm). Round calculations to 4 decimal places. Round your problem solution to 1 decimal place.
Remember, there are 6 cylinders!

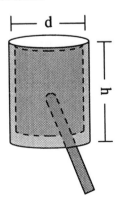

liters (L) = _____

14. An engineering technician is preparing
an estimate for the production of a
special part. The cross-hatched section
of this part will be scrap. Express
the following solutions to 2 decimal
places (rounded).

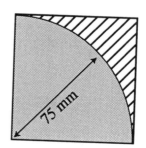

a. What is the area of the square in square millimeters?

a = _____ sq. mm

b. What is the area of the quarter-circle in square millimeters?

b = _____ sq. mm

c. What is the area of the portion to be scraped in square millimeters?

c = _____ sq. mm

d. What is the percentage of waste?

d = _____ %

15. A mechanical engineer must determine the number of meters (m) of belting
required for the conveyor shown here. First find the circumference of each
pulley. Use one-half the circumference of each pulley, then add the distances
between the pulleys.

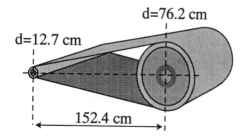

d=76.2 cm

d=12.7 cm

152.4 cm

_____ m

16. The drive pulley on a conveyor system travels at the rate of 20 rpm (revolutions
per minute). The distance of one revolution equals the circumference of the
pulley. How many meters (m) does the conveyor travel in one minute? Your
answer should be in meters (m).

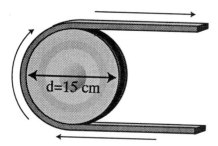

d=15 cm

_____ m

76

17. A powerline technician is preparing a plan for a new right-of-way to shorten the existing line. What is the length of the new line? Use the Pythagorean Theorem to solve this problem, $a^2 + b^2 = c^2$, or in this case, $c^2 - a^2 = b^2$, then find the $\sqrt{}$ of b for length of b. ADD both lengths of b together to get the length of the new line.

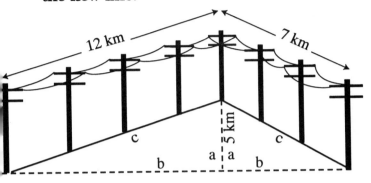

New line = _____ km

18. Another right-of-way is planned for an underground transmission line shown here as side c. What is the length of side c?

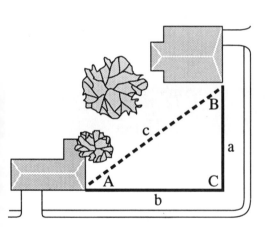

A = 30°

B = 60°

C = 90°

c = _____ km

19. A manufacturer of corrugated shipping cartons reports, that for safety reasons, flat corrugated sheets must not be stacked over 2 meters (m) high when placed on pallets. Corrugated sheets measure 6 mm in thickness. How many sheets of flat corrugated sheets can be stacked safely?

_____ sheets

20. Determine the length of these two proposed transmission line locations.

x = hypotenuse of the right triangle

y = one-quarter arc of a circle with a radius of 2 km

Use the Pythagorean Theorem to find x.
Use a circumference formula to find y.

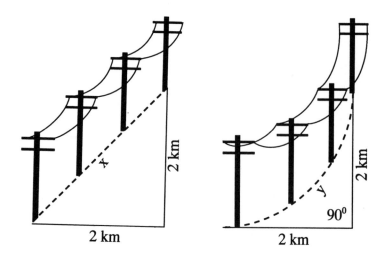

2 km

2 km

90°

2 km

2 km

x = _____ km

y = _____ km

21. A new guy wire is needed to stabilize the
local radio antenna which is 30.5 meters (m)
high. The guy wire is attached to the antenna
1.5 meters (m) below the top. The guy wire
will be anchored 9.15 meters (m) out from the
base of the antenna. How long is the guy-wire?

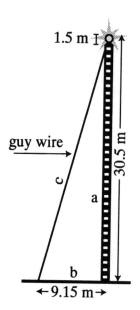

1.5 m

guy wire

c

a

30.5 m

b

←9.15 m→

guy wire = _____ m

22. An automobile wheel including the tire is shown here. The circumference is 30.9 cm. How many turns of the wheel are required to travel 1 km?

$$\text{Turns per km} = \frac{\text{centimeters per km}}{\text{circumference of wheel}}.$$

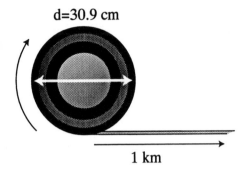

d=30.9 cm

1 km

Total turns = _____

23. A bronze sheeted spire is situated on the ground next to an office building. The base is 3 meters (m) in diameter and rises to a height of 20 meters (m). What is the angle of rise? (Angle A represents the angle of rise.) The spire is shaped like a cone and represents the symbol of strength for this corporation. Use trigonometry to solve this problem.

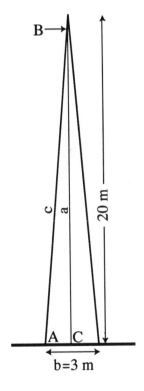

B→

c a 20 m

A C

b=3 m

Angle of rise = _____

24. An engineer for an amusement park is designing a new "Kiddie Thrill Ride". The layout of the flat 2-rail track is shown here. How many meters (m) of the 2-rail track are required? Use the appropriate circumference formula to find the circumference of each circle section. 3 m represents the radius of each circle section. The % represents that portion of the circumference of that particular circle section. ADD all circle sections and straight line segments together to determine the total number of meters (m) required. Round your answer to 2 decimal places.

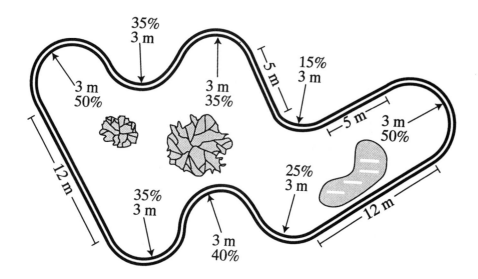

_____ meters (m)

Appendix A

Fraction, Decimal, and Millimeter Equivalents

Fraction	DECIMALS	MILLIMETERS
1/64	0.015625	0.397
1/32	.03125	0.794
3/64	.046875	1.191
1/16	.0625	1.588
5/64	.078125	1.984
3/32	.09375	2.381
7/64	.109375	2.778
1/8	.1250	3.175
9/64	.140625	3.572
5/32	.15625	3.969
11/64	.171875	4.366
3/16	.1875	4.762
13/64	.203125	5.159
7/32	.21875	5.556
15/64	.234375	5.953
1/4	.2500	6.350
17/64	.265625	6.747
9/32	.28125	7.144
19/64	.296875	7.541
5/16	.3125	7.938
21/64	.328125	8.334
11/32	.34375	8.731
23/64	.359375	9.128
3/8	.3750	9.525
25/64	.390625	9.922
13/32	.40625	10.319
27/64	.421875	10.716
7/16	.4375	11.112
29/64	.453125	11.509
15/32	.46875	11.906
31/64	.484375	12.303
1/2	.5000	12.700

Fraction	DECIMALS	MILLIMETERS
33/64	0.515625	13.097
17/32	.53125	13.494
35/64	.546875	13.891
9/16	.5625	14.288
37/64	.578125	14.684
19/32	.59375	15.081
39/64	.609375	15.478
5/8	.6250	15.875
41/64	.640625	16.272
21/32	.65625	16.669
43/64	.671875	17.066
11/16	.6875	17.462
45/64	.703125	17.859
23/32	.71875	18.256
47/64	.734375	18.653
3/4	.7500	19.050
49/64	.765625	19.447
25/32	.78125	19.844
51/64	.796875	20.241
13/16	.8125	20.638
53/64	.828125	21.034
27/32	.84375	21.431
55/64	.859375	21.828
7/8	.8750	22.225
57/64	.890625	22.622
29/32	.90625	23.019
59/64	.921875	23.416
15/16	.9375	23.812
61/64	.953125	24.209
31/32	.96875	24.606
63/64	.984375	25.003
1	1.000	25.400

Table of Common Comparisons

Linear Measure

1 cm	=	0.39 inch
2.54 cm	=	1 inch
1 dm	=	4 inches
3 dm	=	1 foot
1 m	=	39 inches
0.914 m	=	1 yard
1 km	=	0.62 mile
1.62 km	=	1 mile

Area Measure

6.5 sq. cm	=	1 sq. inch
0.09 sq. m	=	1 sq. foot
0.8 sq. m	=	1 sq. yard
2.6 sq. km	=	1 sq. mile
1 sq. cm	=	1.2 sq. yards
1 sq. km	=	0.4 sq. miles

Volume Measure

1 mL	=	0.033 fluid ounces
1 mL	=	0.06 cu. inch
1 L	=	2.113 pints
1 L	=	1.056 quarts
1 L	=	0.264 gallons
1 cu. m	=	35 cu. feet
1 cu. m	=	1.308 cu. yards
1.2 mL	=	1/4 teaspoon
2.5 mL	=	1/2 teaspoon
5 mL	=	1 teaspoon
15 mL	=	1 tablespoon
30 mL	=	1 fluid ounce
120 mL	=	1/2 cup
180 mL	=	3/4 cup
240 mL	=	1 cup
0.473 L	=	1 pint
0.946 L	=	1 quart
3.785 L	=	1 gallon
1 000 mL	=	1 liter
0.03521 cu. m	=	1 cu. foot
0.76 cu. m	=	1 cu. yard

Weight (Mass) Measure

28.35 g	=	1 ounce
0.453 kg	=	1 pound
1 g	=	0.035 ounce
1 kg	=	2.205 pounds

These common comparisons are approximate. They are offered as "time-savers."

Answers

Chapter 1 - Conversions Between Systems

Page 5
1. 3.937 in.
2. 19.62 yds.
3. 4.57 m
4. 15.5 miles
5. 16.09 km
6. 65.6 ft.
7. 275.59 in.
8. 22.05 lbs.
9. 11.355 L
10. 12.7 cm
11. 0.912 m
12. 4.34 miles
13. 39 in.
14. 21.1°C
15. 679.2 g
16. 5.08 dm
17. 2.128 m
18. 10.56 qts.
19. 93.6°F
20. 4.56 m
21. 45.72 cm
22. 3 048 mm
23. 2.972 in.
24. 0.9144 m

Page 6
1. 9.728 m
2. 6.2 mi.
3. 1.20675 km
4. 2.838 L
5. 106.68 cm
6. 339.75 kg
7. 10°C

Page 7
8. 3405 g
9. 93.98 cm
10. 14.791 pts.
11. 16,368 ft.
12. 82 ft.
13. 52.99 L
14. 72 640 g
    72.48 kg

15. 15.24 cm
16. 127 cm

Page 8
17. 86.8 mi.
18. 2 716.8 g
19. 120 sq. ft.
    11.04 sq. m
20. 182.4 m

Chapter 2 - Length Measurements

Page 11
1. 1 000 cm
2. 50 mm
3. 250 mm
4. 0.1 m
5. 0.165 m
6. .000 005 km
7. 500 000 m
8. 0.007 km
9. 7 000 m
10. 0.355 m
11. 7 000 000 m
12. 0.05 hm
13. 0.750 km
14. 15 m
15. 5 000 cm
16. 0.06 km
17. 5 100 mm
18. 3 300 cm
19. 35 000 m
20. 37 500 cm
21. 150 mm
22. 675 mm
23. 3 000 cm
24. 4.9 m
25. 901.5 cm
26. 1 000 cm

Page 12
1.- A = 8 cm
    B = 13 cm
    C = 22 cm
    D = 27 cm
    E = 31 cm
    F = 54 cm
    G = 62 cm
    H = 73 cm
    I = 95 cm
    J = 104 cm

Page 12 - con't
      K = 114 cm
      L = 123 cm
  2.- a. 1.75 cm
      b. 2 mm
      c. 3.81 cm
      d. 10 mm
  3.- a. 50 dm
      b. 500 cm
      c. 5 000 mm
  4.- A = 6 cm
      B = 14 cm
      C = 10 cm
      D = 16 cm

Page 13
  5.- A = 0.9 m
  6.- a. 578 mm
      b. 57.8 cm
      c. 5.78 dm
      d. .578 m
  7. 560 km
  8. Approx. 50 mph
  9. Approx. 350 miles
 10. 560 000 m
 11.-a. 434 cm
      b. 2 455 mm
      c. 10.75 m
      d. 14.91 m

Page 14
      e. 300 020 cm
      f. 545 cm
      g. 5 cm
 12. 2.8956 m
 13. 78.74 in.
 14. 200 cm
 15. 2.01 km
 16. 20 000 m
 17. 5 000 m
 18. 51.488 km
 19. 1.5 m

Page 15
 20. 300 m
 21. 500 m
 22. 567.6 m
 23. 109.44 m
 24. 35.56 cm
 25.-a. 1.6 km
      b. 6 420.48 m

  25.-c. 6 420.48 m
      d. 21,059.174 ft.

Page 16
 25.-e. 401.28 m wide
       802.56 m long
      f. 1 605.12 m
      g. 42,240 ft.

Chapter 3 - Square Measurements
Page 18
  1. 325.5 sq. dm
  2. 80 000 sq. mm
  3. 351 sq. cm

Page 19
  4. 207.5 sq. dm
  5.- a 180 sq. cm
      b. 18 000 sq. mm
      c. 1.8 sq. dm
      d. 0.018 sq. m
  6.- a. 3 sq. m
      b. 300 sq. dm
  7. 4 sq. hm
  8. 5 sq. m
  9. 8 sq. m
 10. 840 sq. m.

Page 20
 11.a. 5.25 sq. m
    b. 78.5 sq. cm
    c. 7.065 sq. dm
    d. 17 662.5 sq. mm
    e. 51 538 sq. cm
 12. 8 000 sq. m
 13. 132.66 sq. m
 14. 116.07 sq. m
 15. 3 200 sq. dm

Page 21
 16. 1 = 6 sq. m
    2 = 6 sq. m
    3 = 12 sq. m
    4 = 2 sq. m
    5 = 12 sq. m
    6 = 24 sq. m
 17- a. 68.64 sq. m
    b. 2 L

Page 22
18. 4 320 sq. m
19. 60 cm x 14 cm or
84 cm x 10 cm
20. 14 sq. m
21. .6 sq. dam
22. 2 400 sq. m

Chapter 4 - Cubic Capacity

Page 24
1. 1 200 cu. dm
2. 1.2 cu. m
3. 0.125 cu. m

Page 25
4.- a. 40 000 cu. cm
b. 1 875 000 cu. cm
c. 800 000 cu. cm
d. 2.715 cu. m
e. 2,715 cu. dm
5. a. 10 cu. dm
b. 5 000 cu. cm
c. 1 000 000 cu. mm

Page 26
6. 630 000 cu. cm
7. 10 007.009 cu. dm
8.- a. 0.007 85 cu. m
b. 0.529 875 cu. m
c. 2 373.84 cu. m

Page 27
9. 2 747.5 cu. m
10. 1 440 cu. m
11. 24 cu. m
12. -a. 1 000 000 cu. mm
b. 225 cu. cm
c. 1.225 cu. dm
d. 1 728 000 cu. mm

Page 28
13.-a. 17.5 cu. m
b. $43.75
14.-a. 4 cu. dm
b 0.018 cu. dm
15.-a. 322 cu. m
b $483.

Page 29
16.-a. 7.8 cu. m
b. 210.6 cu. yds.

17. 1 920 cu. m
18.-a. 3 000 cu. m
b. 3 cu. dam
c. 1 500 000 cu. dm

Page 30
d. 1 200 cu. m
e. 243.84 cu. m
f. 150 cu. m

Chapter 5 - Liquid Capacity

Page 33
1.- a 56.52 cu. m
b. 56 520 L
2.- a. 3 532.5 cu. m
b. 3 532 500 L
3.- a. 753.6 cu. cm
b. .7 536 cu. dm, .7536 L
c. 9.04 L

Page 34
d. 75%
e. 6.78 L
f. 153.68 L
g. $242.76
h. $97.10
4.- a. 1.57 cu. dm
b. 1 570 cu. cm
c. 1.57 L
d. 1.178 L
e. 1.57 kg
f. 1.49 kg
g. 7.85 L

Page 35
5.- a. 3.5325 cu. m
b. 3 532.5 L
c. 1.987 cu. dm
6.- a. 24 L
b. 3 000 L
c. 60 L
d. 450 L
7.- a. 226.08 cu. m
b. .226 08 cu. dam

Page 36
c. 226 080 L
d. 210 254.4 L
e. 346.185 cu. m
f. 346 185 L
g. 242 329.5 L

Page 36 (con't)

  8.- a. 0.398125 cu. m
      b. 398.125 cu. dm
      c. 398.125 L

Page 37

      d. 300 L
      e. 386.18 L
  9.- a .25 cu. m
      b. .375 cu. m
      c. .625 cu. m
      d.-A = 250 L
        B = 375 L
        C = 625 L

Page 38

      e. 937.5 L
  10.-a 900 cu. m
      b. 900 000 L
      c. 90 000 L
      d. 1 400 cu. m
      e. 140 000 L
      f. 55.5%

Chapter 6 - Weight Measurement

Page 40

  1.- a. .000 06 kg
      b. .1 kg
      c. 1.5 kg
      d. 20 kg
      e. 7 kg
      f. .000 005 kg
      g. .012 0 kg
      h. .000 5 kg
      i. .000 005 5 kg
      j. .001 500 kg
      k. .000 25 kg
      l. 108.72 kg

Page 41

  1.- a. 23 547 g
      b. 3 cu. dm
      c. 235 470 dg
  2. Approx. 65 kg

Page 42

  3.- a. 739.3758 kg
      b. 94.2 cu. dm
      c. 739 375.8 g
  4.- a. 6 120 kg
      b. 20 sq. m
      c. 1.2 cu. m

Page 43

  5. 168 cu. m
  6.- a. 376.752 kg
      b.-A = 125.584 kg
        B = 188.376 kg
        C = 62.792 kg
  7. a. .196 25 cu. m
      b. 196.25 L
        196.25 kg
      c. 49 L

Page 44

  8.- a = 109.98 kg
      b. = 295 hg
      c. = 195 kg
      d. = 10.15 g
  9.- a 187.5 kg
      b. 187.5 cu. dm
      c. 187 500 g
  10.-a. 12.32 kg

Page 45

  11.-a. 84 kg
      b. 42 000 g
  12.-a. 2 610.125 cu. m
      b. 73 732.34 bu.
      c. 71 520.37 bu.
      d. 2 005 519.65 kg
      e. 2 610 124.84 L
      f. 2 218 606.11 L

Chapter 7 - Temperature Measurement

Page 48

  1. 29°C
  2.- Answers to nearest tenth:
      a. 10°C
      b. 23.9°C
      c. 65.6°C
      d. -2.8°C
      e. 79.4°C
      f. 18.3°C
      g. -9.4°C
      h. 100°C
      i. 32.2°C
      j. 37.8°C
      k. 2.8°C

Page 49

  3.- a. 22.4°C
      b. 24°C

Page 49 (con't)

    c. 20.8°C
    d. 25.6°C
    e. 23.2°C
    f. 22.4°C
    g. 24°C
    h. 23.2°C
3.- a. 10°C
    b. 23.8°C
    c. 65.5°C
    d. -2.7°C
    e. 79.4°C
    f. 18.3°C
    g. -9.4°C
    h. 100°C
    i. 32.2°C
    j. 37.7°C
    k. 2.8°C
4.- a. 149°C
    b. 163°C
    c. 177°C
    d. 135°C
    e. 121°C
    f. 107°C
5. 22.2°C
6. 37°C

Page 50

7. 82.2°C
8. 38.3°C
9. 50°C
10. 52.7°C
11. 47.7°C
12. 13.9°C

Page 51

13.-a. 25 hrs.
    b. 2 hrs.
    c. 4 hrs.
    d. 5 hrs.
14.-a. 126.7°C
    b. 154.4°C
    c. 356°F
    d. 210°C
    e. 428°F
    f. 320°F
    g. 107.2°C
    h. 246.1°C
    i. 446°F
    j. 311°F
    k. 374°F
    l. 218.3°F

14.-m.198.9°F
    n. 338°F
    o. 293°F

Page 52

15. 10°C
16. 8.3°C
17. 11.1°C

Chapter 8 - Metrics & Percents

Page 54

.741 = 74.1%
.29 = 29%
1.25 = 125%
$\frac{4}{4}$ = 100%
$\frac{4}{20}$ = 20%
$\frac{1}{4}$ = 25%
$\frac{55}{100}$ = $\frac{11}{20}$ = 55%

Page 59

1. 20%
2. 15
3. 60
4. 16.7%
5. $160.
6. 21.6%
7. $1086

Page 60

8. $62,500.
9. 11.5%
10. $56.25
11. 11.1%
12. 120 sq. m
13. 72 sq. m
14. 14.4 sq. m gr. beans
    10.8 sq. m corn

Page 61

15. 4 008 sq. m
16. 601 cu. m
17. 60.1 cu. m
18. 20%
19. 25%
20. 1.88 m

Page 62
 21. 1.84 m
 22. 6.25%
 23. 25%
 24. 21.4%
 25. 15 cm
 26. 59.055"
 27. 6.2 miles
 28. 172.431 lbs.

Page 63
 29. 58.65 kg
 30. 0.0914 km

Chapter 9 - Combination Problems

Page 65
 1.- a. 100 cm
   b. 3 532.05 kg
 2.- a. 2.977 sq. m
   b. 400

Page 66
   c. 72 sq. cm
   d. 968 sq. cm
 3.- a. 225 sq. dm
   b. 78.5 sq. dm
 4.- A = 28 sq. cm
   B = .36 sq. dm
   C = 1 800 sq. mm
 5. 2.432 m

Page 67
 6.- a. 1.259 m
   b. 98.5 dm
   c. 396 cm
   d. 4 000 g
   e. 15 dm
   f. 100 mm
   g. 125 000 cm
   h. 96 cm
   i. 115 mg
   j. 5 cg
   k. .95 dm
   l. 1505 m
   m. 60 dm
   n. 2001.005 L
   o. 6.15 dm
 7.- A = 55 cm
   B = 3 cm

 7.- C = 3 cm
   D = 5 cm
   E = 11 cm
   F = 12 cm
   G = 9 cm
   H = 10 cm
   I = 16 cm
   J = 29 cm
   K = 64 cm

Page 68
 8.- a. 1.9625 cu. dm
   b. 1.57 dm
 9.- a. 1 cu. m
   b. 1 000 kg
 10.-a. 3 000 cu. dm
   b. 8

Page 69
 11.-a. 50 sq. hm
   b. 500 sq. dam
   c. 5 000 sq. m
   d. 50 000 sq. dm
   e. 500 000 sq. cm
 12.-a. 200 km
   b. 4 hrs. 30 min.
   c. 70 km/hr.
   d. 4 min.
 13. 453.6 g
 14. 45 mL
 15. 329°F

Page 70
 16. 152.4 cm
 17. 45.3 kg
 18. 1312 ft.
 19. 182.4 m long
   91.2 m wide
 20. 2 006.4 m
 21. 1.976 m

Chapter 10 - Metrics and Technology

Page 73
 1. A = 55° 9'
 2. b = 8.03
 3. a = 11.468
 4. c = 13.948
 5. a = 0.6018
   b = 0.8572

Page 73 (con't)
      c = 1.2349
      d = 31
      e = 33
      f = 5
  6. 144 sq. m

Page 74
  7. B = 2° 27'
  8. 11 790 cu. m
  9. B = 36° 52' 12"
      A = 53° 7' 48"
      c = 15
 10. 86 137 sq. cm

Page 75
 11. ∠ B = 123° 15'
      P = 482 m
 12. P = 1 225.81 cm
      A = 77 670.81 sq. cm
 13. L = 2.8

Page 76
 14. a = 5 625 sq. mm
      b = 4 415.63 sq. mm
      c = 1 209.37 sq. mm
      d = 21.5%
 15. 4.4437 m
 16. 9.42 m

Page 77
 17. New line = 15.8 km
 18. c = 4 km
 19. 333 sheets

Page 78
 20. x = 2.828 km
      y = 3.14 km
 21. guy wire = 30.41 m

Page 79
 22. Total turns = 3,229.104
 23. Angle of rise = 85° 42' 39"

Page 80
 24. 87.69 m

269